250-51

THE
COMMUNITY
IS
THE
CLASSROOM

THE COMMUNITY IS THE CLASSROOM

MARTHA IRWIN
and
WILMA RUSSELL

PENDELL
PUBLISHING
COMPANY

PENDELL
PUBLISHING
COMPANY

International Standard Book Number: 0-87812-014-9
Library of Congress Catalog Card Number: 79-168585

To

Larry and Terry
Kirk, Gregg, Angie, and Kim
and all of the other young citizens
who would benefit
from a community-centered curriculum

CONTENTS

CONTENTS (Cont'd)

CONTENTS (Cont'd)

LIST OF FIGURES

PREFACE

As children and adults face the realities of living, they do not consider whether they are using special reading skills or basing their decisions upon knowledge from biochemistry. Rather, they meet situations as they perceive them and attempt solutions as best they can in light of all of their past experiences. In school, however, the skills and the knowledge are often seen as ends in themselves, with the implicit assumption by educators and lay people that the sequential development of skills and the acquisition of bits of compartmentalized information will prepare pupils for more effective participation in society. Still working on that assumption, many proponents of innovational instructional programs are concentrating on technology and rigid courses of study to prepare students to meet the increasingly complex needs of human existence. The pleas of students for programs that make sense and their antagonism toward spending several hours each week in an institution that is more concerned with imparting trivia than with fostering human relationships should convince us that the assumption is untenable. The fostering of human relationships for effective personal growth and social participation in everyday living in the real world does indeed depend upon the ability of citizens to use skills and knowledge. But why not gain these requisites in an open classroom that is community centered—a classroom in which study skills and knowledge from all relevant disciplines are learned and used as needed to solve problems appropriate to the pupils?

We believe that functional skills, integration of content, and social sensitivity are achieved best in an instructional program that utilizes the community as a classroom and provides an open environment for learning. Furthermore, we believe that experimentation with one organizational scheme after another and the formation of endless curriculum committees to select the most recently packaged materials must be supplanted by preparation and inservice programs that will help teachers to become oriented to a community-centered curriculum.

ACKNOWLEDGMENTS

Our thanks go to all of those educators who made our school and museum visits possible. We wish to acknowledge especially the following people and their staffs: Mrs. A. J. Dean, Primary Education Adviser, Berkshire, England; Miss Winifred Hickson, Inspector of Schools, Bristol, England; Mr. Peter W. Young, Senior Inspector for Primary Schools, Leicester, England; Mr. Leslie Jackman, Schools Museum Officer, Torquay Museum of Natural History, Torquay, England; and Mr. Michael Wyatt Wheeler, Schools Museum Officer, The Bowes Museum, Barnard Castle County, England. We also wish to acknowledge the assistance of the following people in helping us to obtain illustrative photographs: Mrs. Jane A. Rehberg, Inkster Public Schools, Inkster, Michigan; Mr. H. Robert Cracknell, Warren Consolidated Schools, Warren, Michigan; and Mr. Samuel LoPresto, Van Buren Public Schools, Belleville, Michigan. We wish to thank Gregory T. Patton for drawing to scale our plans for a learning laboratory.

CHAPTER I

**AREAS OF CONCERN
IN THE
CURRENT EDUCATIONAL SCENE**

Areas of Concern in the
Current Educational Scene

The community is a classroom. Children are learning as they live. The natural learning environment is a rich one indeed, yet today many children are experiencing difficulty with a school curriculum which makes limited use of this valuable resource. A major problem in education is that present-day instructional programs are not related to children's home and community experiences. For many children the community and the classroom are two different, unrelated worlds. Perhaps these two worlds can become one if the community is used effectively and extensively as a learning laboratory.

The attainment of an integrated curriculum in which the community is a learning laboratory need not be an ivory tower conceptualization. Much can be accomplished by teachers who are committed to perfecting some of the approaches which have long been advocated and supported by sound principles of learning. Although unit teaching has been widely accepted in theory, it has not yet been fully implemented in the classroom. Teachers have not involved students in decision-making and cooperative planning, despite long years of lip service to these pedagogical constructs. Very few teachers and pupils—even those functioning in open classrooms—have engaged in integrated studies evolving from problems of deep concern in the local community. Teachers must become familiar with the resources

3

in their local areas and with the use of these resources in planned learning experiences. By using the realities of the community as starting points for study, pupils will find meaning in subject matter, realize a need to acquire skills, and experience an integrated curriculum.

Using the community as a classroom has potential for bringing about improvement in many of the areas of concern in the current educational scene. Some of these concerns are: improving instructional programs for the educationally disadvantaged, individualizing instruction, building positive self-concepts, providing opportunities for creative expression, increasing perceptual awareness, developing problem-solving skills, involving students in curriculum planning, fostering language and concept development, encouraging social sensitivity, and weaving all of these together into a relevant curriculum.

INSTRUCTIONAL PROGRAMS FOR THE EDUCATIONALLY DISADVANTAGED

The fact that large groups of educationally disadvantaged children have been identified is one indication that educators have not related school programs to the backgrounds and interests of their learners. [1] Most schools have a middle-class value orientation and most college programs have not prepared teachers to relate to inner-city children and their needs.

Current searches for materials and techniques for teaching the disadvantaged tend to be centered on substantive areas and skills. However, focusing on knowledge and skills is not sufficient. If the instructional program is to benefit individuals and society, educators must be concerned with appreciations, attitudes, and social understandings as well. Furthermore, knowledge and skills are best learned and applied in meaningful, purposeful settings. Yet, for many students, the content, setting, and processes of learning are almost totally irrelevant and meaningless. The expected learnings are often unrelated to one another as well as to the experiences of the students.

[1] This statement can be documented in the Coleman and Kerner reports. The *Report of the National Advisory Commission on Civil Disorders* (New York: New York Times Co., 1968) is generally referred to as the "Kerner Report." *Equality of Educational Opportunity* (U.S. Department of Health, Education and Welfare, Office of Education, 1966) is generally referred to as the "Coleman Report."

Poverty situations, dialect differences, and lack of school-related experiential backgrounds contribute to difficulties for many children. The difficulties begin in the early school years and are compounded as students either struggle to maintain contact with the school's formal program or drop out physically or psychologically.

Further difficulties arise because of insufficient funds for instructional purposes and because of an inequitable distribution of the funds that are available. In this country, children do not have equal educational opportunities in terms of materials, facilities, professional personnel, and class size.

Many suburban children are also deprived of an adequate education. Children in suburban schools are often so isolated that they and their teachers have little contact with different social values and multi-cultural views. As a result they lack social awareness and social sensitivity.[2]

INDIVIDUALIZING INSTRUCTION

Individualizing instruction poses another crucial problem for educators today. The traditional school provides for group instruction with a class size of approximately twenty-five to thirty-five pupils per teacher. Group instruction is usually accompanied by grade-level expectations and by grade-level standards of achievement. The competitive marking system which results perpetuates adherence to standards, militates against provisions for individual development, and creates psychological problems. Hence individual differences in learning are not valued.

Some attempts to break the lock-step in education have been made in recent years. An increased use of programmed instruction is one example. But programmed instruction carried out in carrels and learning booths permits very little social interaction among pupils or between pupils and the teacher. Most programs and multi-media packages focus on the acquisition of facts and make no provisions for children to ask questions or to respond creatively. Furthermore, the subject content is organized in a pre-determined, logical sequence by program writers who do not even know the learners.

Some other attempts to break the lock-step have included the reorganization of the textbook around units of study and the use of multiple texts and

---

[2] This conclusion is supported by the study done by Alice Miel with Edwin Kiester, Jr., as reported in *The Shortchanged Children of Suburbia* (New York: Institute of Human Relations Press, The American Jewish Committee, 1967).

other supplementary materials of varying levels. In certain schools an ungraded curriculum has been developed which allows for the continuous progress of the learners. Most of these attempts to individualize instruction have not gone far enough. Current programs have not been planned around the experiences of individual learners, and the curriculum has not been made relevant to space age children growing up in a rapidly changing society.

If improvement is to come in our schools, provisions must be made for each child to develop to his potential as he uses subject content to interact with persons and things in his environment. To promote such interaction, the teacher must serve as a resource and a facilitator of learning. The focus must be on the learning environment rather than on the teaching act and the subject content.

A POSITIVE SELF-CONCEPT

Many children today lack positive feelings about themselves. They are seeking identity, personal meaning, worth, and dignity as human beings. Some children labelled as educationally disadvantaged are "problems" because they have been unable to identify with a school program which is remote from their living experiences. Their family structures and out-of-school activities are different from those described in the textbooks, and their home backgrounds are viewed as inconsequential in relation to the topics discussed in the classroom.

The self-concept is enhanced when one has established satisfying relationships with others. The child needs to feel he is accepted by his peer group, his teachers, and other adults in the instructional environment. The nonverbal behavior of these significant others may be far more important than their verbal behavior. In any case, the learner is keenly aware of the feedback he receives in his efforts to establish positive relationships. [3]

A child's feeling of worth is also enhanced when he experiences success in school; however, failure for many children is built in to some of the

---

[3] Note the self-fulfilling prophecy as revealed in the Rosenthal and Jacobson studies. Robert Rosenthal and Lenore Jacobson, *Pygmalion in the Classroom* (New York: Holt, Rinehart and Winston, Inc., 1968).

common school practices. LaBenne and Greene indicate that practices in grading, promotion, grouping, and classroom management are often destructive and do little to foster the worth and dignity of the individual.[4]

OPPORTUNITIES FOR CREATIVE EXPRESSION

In school the emphasis is usually on right answers—the accumulation of factual information. Convergent thinking is emphasized, and a closed rather than an open learning environment is created. A single standard of achievement based on class and group goals encourages conformity. A curriculum so narrowly defined limits the opportunities to deviate from organized plans and stifles creativity.

While it is true that creativity can be nurtured in all areas of the curriculum, teachers frequently limit their ideas about creative expression to the fields of art and music. Some classroom activities carried out under the label of creativity are nothing more than patterned exercises, as is the case with the teacher who asks the children to draw three red trucks from the example she has supplied. Often teachers do not realize they are negating their art program when they provide structured seatwork assignments in the form of dittoed outlines for children to color.[5] Creativity in music is limited, too, when teachers force children to march in step in order to develop rhythmic sensitivity. Opportunities for creativity exist in all aspects of the instructional program. For example, divergent thinking could be encouraged if teachers were to ask children to solve math problems in as many different ways as possible.

In addition to curricular problems, limited opportunities for creativity can have psychological effects. Because of his tendencies toward divergent thinking and non-conformity, the creative child is frequently not recognized or accepted by his peer group or by his teachers. He may find it difficult to establish satisfying relationships with his classmates. An even greater problem is that the creative child may be a threat to his teacher; subsequently, many children repress divergent inclinations and the resultant loss of original thinkers is detrimental to society.

[4] Wallace D. LaBenne and Bert I. Greene, *Educational Implications of Self-Concept Theory* (Pacific Palisades, California: Goodyear Publishing Co., Inc., 1969).

[5] Professor Alice Keliher referred to these as "purple passion sheets" in her address, "Directions in Early Childhood Education," to the Department of Elementary School Principals, National Education Association, in 1967.

The creativity of children is somewhat related to the creativity of their teachers. Unfortunately many teachers who could be innovative have limited opportunities to plan more flexible instructional programs. They function within a framework which rewards conformity and prevents them from experimenting with something new. It is also true that some teachers who function in a less restrictive climate may lack the skills to create a more open learning environment.

DEVELOPMENT OF PERCEPTUAL AWARENESS

Children see relationships that the school does not see — or think important. As children engage in their daily activities they are aware of significant aspects of their environment that are not included in the educational program. Because of their interests and their points of view, children are concerned with objects and situations that escape the attention of school personnel, and if their repeated efforts to raise questions are rebuffed, pupils quickly learn that curiosity is not valued in school.

Children's perceptions are significant to them and they must be accepted and valued by educators. Many adults do not have the sensitivity to relate to children and to understand their interests; they seem to care little about reactions that may lead away from the planned lesson content. As a result, pupils may be reluctant to share their perceptions about any topic.

When teachers do all of the planning for classroom activities, problems of motivation arise. Teachers who attempt to force their perceptions upon pupils become frustrated in their efforts to motivate learning. On the other hand, if children are encouraged to share perceptions about the area for study and to participate in setting goals, they will be motivated and, consequently, more meaningful learning experiences will result.

Recently much attention has been focused upon the development of perceptual awareness, but teachers have usually limited their concern to the development of auditory and visual discrimination. However, depth of perception depends upon a wide range of sensory experiences which include touch, smell, sound, taste and sight, and even more important than these sensory contacts are the meanings attached to them. Educators must be concerned with such questions as: How do the child's sensory experiences help him to recall his past? How do they lead him to new experiences? How does perceptual awareness help the child to understand human behavior? As teachers begin to understand the importance of these kinds of questions, perhaps they will encourage children to share perceptions and attach meaning to them.

Teachers also have the responsibility for helping children to develop new insights into elements of their world which they have thus far perceived only slightly or not at all. A bare classroom has little to perceive. A child's curiosity is not excited in a setting characterized by dated texts, poorly planned bulletin boards, and orderly rows of desks symmetrically aligned before the teacher's station. The current attention given to developing perceptual sensitivity is too frequently centered around formal, programmed materials—learning to be acquired via the workbook. Perceptual awareness can be encouraged only in an environment that is rich in learning stimuli.

PROBLEM-SOLVING SKILLS

In many of our schools today, the wrong people are asking the questions and children are placed in the position of supplying answers to questions they would like to ignore. Artificially created learning situations in which students answer the questions at the end of the chapter and fill in the blanks in the workbook or other programmed material reveal that some teachers are more concerned with the acquisition of factual information than with the development of critical thinking and problem-solving skills. Teachers invariably include the development of problem-solving skills in statements of objectives. They agree that these are essential goals, but give little attention to them in the instructional program. The reason for this neglect is that many teachers do not understand the real meaning of problem-solving and its implications for school programs.

In most classrooms students have few opportunities to identify a problem, to move through the steps toward a solution, and to evaluate their efforts. They are not encouraged to raise questions, and if questions do arise, children do not know how to seek answers; furthermore, they are often unaware that they *should* seek answers or that their questions are important. Children have learned that their spontaneous questions are not to be considered a part of the formal program of the school.

Young people are criticized because they do not assume responsibility and do not develop good study skills. However, until the schools involve students in determining goals and assuming responsibility for achieving them, the acquisition of problem-solving abilities will not become an integral part of their educational program.

STUDENT INVOLVEMENT IN CURRICULUM PLANNING

Traditionally pupils have been quite limited in expressing and pursuing their interests to the extent that relationships between school activities and outside interests seem non-existent. Because students have not been involved, they have been unable to become self-directive or to share in decision-making.

The curriculum has been planned by adults who hold the long-range goal of preparing children for participation later in an adult society. They view children as citizens of the future but fail to recognize that youngsters are already participating citizens in today's world. The ever-recurring conflict between youth and adults indicates what happens under such circumstances— young people seek involvement, they identify problems, and then find they lack the opportunity or experience to move toward solutions.

The inability of teachers to involve students in curriculum planning may be a result of the teachers' own inexperience. If they have not shared in decision-making with administrators, they will likely have misconceptions about the meaning of student involvement.

Added problems arise when teachers consider physical activity synonymous with learning by doing. In those classrooms where children are given almost complete freedom to pursue their own interests, teachers have failed to assume their roles as adults. They have been unable to recognize their major responsibility for helping students develop skills of planning, organizing, and evaluating learning activities.

LANGUAGE AND CONCEPT DEVELOPMENT

Some children cannot communicate with teachers and some teachers cannot communicate with children. The language the child brings to school may not be acceptable because the teacher's middle-class vocabulary, language, and values get in the way of understanding, and consequently both the teacher and learner have misconceptions about what is being said. In such a climate there is no provision for the many different vocabulary and language patterns that prevail, nor is there an appreciation of standard and nonstandard dialects.

Another problem with language and concept development is that the traditional emphasis upon grammar has not led to the improvement of communication skills. Too often it has led to a school program that encourages concentration upon the mechanics of composition and places

10

an emphasis upon rote learning. Thus the teacher and child do not communicate and the teacher fails to discover concepts the child has already formed; instead he resorts to the teacher-directed approach of the conventional classroom.

Real concept development, that which extends beyond verbalization, depends upon experience. Most schools limit firsthand experiences and rely instead upon textbook lessons and recitations. Films and other audio-visual materials are rarely used to provide well-planned vicarious experiences. When concepts are not developed in a variety of settings with a multi-media approach, depth and breadth of meaning are not ensured.

Teachers have attempted to present concepts through a logically organized series of lessons which may be "logical" to everyone but the learner. Ideally the learning sequence should proceed from the direct to the more abstract, but in many school learning experiences the sequence is just the reverse. Children read stories about life in the country, see a film or filmstrip, discuss rural occupations, and eventually they may visit a farm. Unfortunately it is only at the end of the study that the child has some firsthand experience. Another "logically" organized sequence is illustrated by the chronological teaching of history. Many educators are now recommending that the study of history should begin with present-day concerns, and historical events should be considered as they relate to current problems. Above all, the organization of content should be logical to the learner and a variety of activities should be provided for adequate concept development.

SOCIAL SENSITIVITY

The restricted environment of the traditional school provides limited opportunity for the development of social sensitivity. Because of the "We don't talk in school" attitude, human interaction is curbed. The usual classroom setting encourages the isolation of learners and creates a barrier between the learners and the teacher.

Multi-cultural values are rarely recognized when the student population comes from the same social milieu. For example, a suburban student body may be almost totally unaware of differing values and ways of living in the inner-city area. Exchange programs designed to improve this situation frequently fail because of community resistance. In a school in which the student body does represent a wider range of cultural values, educators often attempt to form ability groups for instructional purposes with the result that social isolation continues. Even when learners are grouped by age as in the traditional grade levels, they are quite limited in their contacts

11

with older and younger children. Since any form of grouping places restrictions upon human interaction, the criteria for establishing groups must be considered very carefully.

Few planned and guided experiences are provided by the school to develop social awareness. Most school programs do not encourage young people to participate in social service projects in the community. Within the school itself, participation in the student activity program should promote social sensitivity, but many of these programs are not representative of the entire student body and only offer prestige to youth who already have status.

Children acquire their patterns of social behavior through identification and emulation, and the teacher's impact as a social model is often underestimated. While some teachers are deeply concerned about their verbal behavior in the classroom, they fail to realize that the nonverbal behavior is even more critical in fostering human relationships. Children feel the acceptance or rejection of their teachers, and the teacher who understands these feelings will strive to create a warm, friendly learning environment.

A RELEVANT CURRICULUM

The overarching concern in this chapter is that present-day instructional programs are not related to children's home and community experiences. This situation exists because the traditional school has not been responsive to present-day problems, but instead has been concerned with organizational patterns and the establishment of academic standards. Educators have been searching for a panacea or an instant packaged solution, a ready-made-curriculum-in-a-box. Solutions to curriculum problems are not so simple nor are they so quickly achieved.

A relevant curriculum will result if children become involved in meaningful activities which relate in-school and out-of-school experiences. Children learn as they live in an open classroom which serves as a coordinating center for that larger learning laboratory — the expanding community. A community-centered curriculum utilizing the natural learning environment has much potential for the future of education, and the remaining chapters of this book contain suggestions for the implementation of such a program.

CHAPTER II

**CHARACTERISTICS
OF A
COMMUNITY-CENTERED CURRICULUM**

Characteristics of a Community-Centered Curriculum

The community is a laboratory for learning. In this laboratory children interact with their environment and their first and most enduring learnings occur. The community-centered curriculum is an extension of the natural learning environment, with the classroom serving as a coordinating center for a variety of experiences that reach out into the expanding community. Thus the child's in-school experiences and out-of-school experiences are one and the same. The content of the curriculum, centering around life in the community and community problems, encompasses a multidisciplinary approach and requires a wise utilization of resources.

THE LEARNING LABORATORY

The learning laboratory of the community-centered school may be viewed as a concentric circle with the *classroom* as the focal point of activity. The *school* as an instructional resource center occupies the surrounding area, and the *community* with its natural setting for learning lies beyond. Stimuli for learning can originate in any of the areas, however, the most meaningful questions are likely to arise as a result of children's direct experiences in the community.

The Learning Laboratory

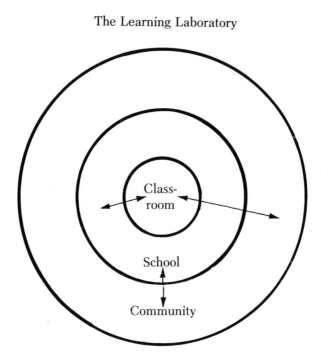

Firsthand experiences in the community should be used as initiatory and continuing activities, to be reinforced by the resources available in the classroom and the school. Some of the experiences which stimulate learning in the local community and in the community-centered school are: observing, asking questions, seeking information, testing hypotheses, experimenting, and evaluating findings. Engaged in these activities, learners are far removed from the passive roles they have assumed in the traditional school. The teacher's role is that of an active participant with the learners, the adult who guides and facilitates, the primary resource in helping children to reach their objectives as they develop learning skills. The children are stimulated to move from the known to the unknown as they participate in activities in the classroom, the school, and the community.

The classroom should be the learning laboratory where children coordinate the activities they are carrying out in their community.
Courtesy Van Buren Public Schools, Belleville, Michigan.

The Classroom as an Enriched Environment

If the community is the learning laboratory, the classroom is the coordinating center of that laboratory and must provide an enriched environment. The classroom should have movable furniture, ample storage space, materials readily accessible, bulletin boards and shelves for displays—a generally cheery, uncluttered setting that engenders security for the learners. Two types of learning centers are desirable in the classroom: work areas and centers of interest. Some activities are common to both centers, but generally work areas provide children with opportunities to gather in groups for discussing, writing, viewing pictures, and working cooperatively on projects. Centers of interest, on the other hand, are usually developed around science, music, reading, and social studies, and in these spaces interesting displays, models, and realia from the community are exhibited.

To benefit from this physically enriched environment, children must develop self-direction in making use of the resources available. Students must be

17

involved as work patterns are established and evaluated if responsible freedom is to become a reality.

Creating an enriched environment in an open classroom poses problem-solving situations for the learners, involves them in some creative endeavors, and encourages them to develop social skills. For example, the teacher and students might begin by considering such questions as: How can we make our classroom more attractive? What is the role of the Board of Education in providing adequate facilities? Why are funds limited? How can pupils become involved in bringing about change? Finding answers to such questions as these could lead to the study of a problem which draws content from many subject fields and makes use of an integrated approach to learning.

The School as an Instructional Resource Center

The school and its environs provide countless opportunities for firsthand learning experiences. Because of geographic location or density of population, this environment may be so restricted that it includes only the building and its enclosed grounds. But even within this limited area are many untapped physical and human resources.

The entire school should be considered as a resource center. Some of the physical resources that can provide learning experiences are the cafeteria, playground, public address system, and power plant. Special resource people in the school might include the custodian, cook, school secretary, school nurse, and principal. Without ever leaving the building, students can study electricity, machines, textures, shapes, services, roles, functions, and power figures. They can become increasingly aware that the ongoing school program depends upon all of the interrelated units functioning together as a whole. The school as a circumscribed community can be examined in relation to the local community and the expanding world community.

Although the entire school contains stimuli for learning, special areas should be designated for resources and activities. The library in many schools has been expanded into an instructional materials center. Ideally, classrooms should be located around an instructional resource center so that learners will have ready access to the materials and an open environment for learning will be created. The instructional resource center can be viewed as broader in scope than the traditional school library and should have printed materials consisting of books, including paperbacks, picture collections, newspapers, magazines, pamphlets, brochures, and files of resource materials collected and produced by teachers and students. In addition to printed materials,

The richness of the classroom environment is determined by the opportunities for children to explore and interact rather than by the cost of the equipment. The enrichment might begin simply by pushing two desks over to the chalkboard, adding a filmstrip previewer, and allowing children to write stories when they wish or *if* they wish.

Children who are involved in planning a more flexibly arranged classroom and in establishing and evaluating work patterns soon become self-directive in moving about and working together.

When children are encouraged to communicate about their own experiences using their language and choice of media, the writing center will be a gathering place for earnest young authors.

A typewriter can be a valuable "teaching machine" for any age. The learning possibilities range from getting acquainted with letters, to learning to spell, and to investigating the construction and mechanics of this piece of equipment.

Scrap lumber and very simple blocks can be used to improve coordination and to stimulate perceptual learnings.

Blocks can become the framework for a garage, bus, space ship, or a club house where boys can relive field trips, re-create events seen on television, or engage in imaginative adventures.

Kindergarten children are quite serious as they try out societal roles in a house corner. If primary teachers were to continue to provide for dramatic play, the children would become increasingly self-directed and responsible as they relate to others.

A first science center might be as simple as a gerbil in a cage, established and maintained as a result of teacher-pupil planning and evaluation.

the center also should contain realia, models, reproductions, tapes, films, filmstrips, transparencies, and equipment for their use. Still cameras and movie cameras should be accessible so that students can make their own photographs, slides, and films.

These resources should be organized in a large area which has both open space and small work centers. If the large open space is carpeted and if a portion of it is designed as a theater-in-the-round, it can be used by teachers, students, and the community for a variety of activities, such as storytelling, dramatic play, lectures, and large group discussions of the town-meeting type. Small work areas are needed for special projects such as a darkroom for developing photographs, rooms for arts and crafts activities, and places for small groups to meet.

An open environment implies freedom for children to use the resources of the school constructively, and challenges the teacher to work creatively with children, colleagues, aides, student teachers, and administrative personnel. The open environment created in an instructional resource center will provide excellent opportunities for human interaction, inasmuch as the teacher and pupils will be able to work with all school personnel freely as needs arise.

Even though an ideal resource center has been described, it is fully recognized that conditions other than the ideal prevail in most schools. Many of the materials and activities found in the instructional resource center can be provided in the traditional school setting, but some modification may be made depending upon the ingenuity of the teacher. For example, children's own drawings can be made into a roller movie. Cameras can be borrowed and, even though an elementary school lacks a dark room, members of a high school photography club might welcome the experience of cooperating with elementary youngsters. Teachers and pupils can scout around the building for unused materials. A book storage closet may yield old basal readers from which stories can be extracted, creatively rebound, and used for individualized reading. More equipment is available in most schools and communities than is ever identified and used.

The Community as a Natural Setting for Learning

Learning must extend beyond the classroom and the school in order for the students to understand the complexities of a modern day society. Since the child spends only a portion of his day within the confines of the school,

Somehow reading is more fun when you can sit on the floor and can read together if you wish. Whether in the instructional materials center or in the classroom, books are more inviting if the fronts are exposed.
Courtesy Inkster Public Schools, Inkster, Michigan.

In an open environment, more opportunities are available for a teacher or another resource person to introduce a group of children to a new media such as potato printing.
Courtesy Warren Consolidated Schools, Warren, Michigan.

Photographs of children are excellent inspirations for language arts activities. A camera and a portable tape recorder will help children bring their community experiences back into their learning laboratory, too.

An inexpensive camera and the assistance of a high school photography club or a local amateur dark room artist are invaluable for their contributions to the enhancement of positive self-concepts.

which, because of its very nature is a limited environment, it is the school's responsibility to help the child view the community in its total operation. The school as an educational institution is restricted to a limited physical setting, specially designated age groups, and school-oriented services.

Beyond the restricted school setting is the home environment of each learner. Activities of families and of children themselves are replete with interrelated learnings which naturally encompass many of the content areas and developmental skills. Photographs brought from home may be used in the classroom. A simple picture such as a kitten on a ledge may stimulate creative writing or story telling. Encouraging children to take pictures of activities or scenes of interest to them may provide the stimulus for in-depth studies which appeal to learners.

The learning laboratory for any community-centered curriculum includes the resources available within the school and community: businesses, industries, government offices, civic organizations, religious institutions, museums, historical sites, and community services. Every citizen, both adult and child, has the potential for contributing to the instructional program.

The local environment can be used as a setting to stimulate children to ask questions and develop new interests. Their study of the local area will lead inevitably to a consideration of regional and world relationships. For example, in studying the grocery store and its operation, children are soon grappling with problems of transportation and trade that have regional and world-wide implications. Many of the basic understandings or generalizations regarding interpersonal relationships and man's interaction with his environment may be learned because they are illustrated as effectively in the local area as in the world community.

The firsthand experience of children viewing erosion in the community might develop into a study of a local community problem that has world-wide implications. Children's interests and concerns about erosion may be quite artificial if teachers try to stimulate them in the classroom, but direct contact with the problem leads to questions from the children, the use of additional resources, and in-depth study. Audio-visual and printed materials of the school are then used as the need for more information becomes apparent.

When learning activities occur in a setting in which the classroom, the school, and the community function together, the ideal of the community-centered curriculum can be realized.

With increased perceptual awareness, teachers will realize that there are a multitude of learning possibilities within a block of any classroom regardless of its location. In the area represented in this photo, children could study street signs, parking meters, traffic patterns, car designs, geometric shapes, and building materials. They could hypothesize about the snow that remains near the bushes. Interest in the water tower could lead children to considerations of architectural styles, water storage and distribution systems, and local governmental services and costs. A public opinion survey about this historic landmark would help students gain an awareness of the attitudes and values of long-time residents and of newcomers. A university professor might take a class of future teachers out of the college classroom to stir creative thinking about the learning possibilities within the shadow of the ivory tower. A principal might exercise curriculum leadership by holding a series of "walking staff meetings" on the lawn, the playground, and one block in each direction from the school building. Indeed, the community is the classroom.

THE INTEGRATED CURRICULUM

An integrated curriculum can become a reality in the natural setting for learning which the community provides. However, the setting in and of itself will not be sufficient to ensure change. The teacher must implement a program which draws upon content from many disciplines, provides opportunities for pupils to develop learning skills, promotes attitudes conducive to mental health, and encourages creativity. Because this is not the instructional pattern in most schools, teachers may find it desirable to use a gradual approach to initiate change from a traditional to an integrated curriculum. One sequence for change is to move from the traditional use of the textbook to an inquiry approach, which can then be expanded into topic-centered instruction. As teachers become more flexible and experienced, a unit method may be employed, to lead into a program of fully integrated studies. The model is designed to indicate that these approaches form a graduated sequence. Each step is more advanced than the one preceding because it includes a wider range of experiences and a more flexible use of resources.

Instructional Patterns Leading
To An Integrated Curriculum

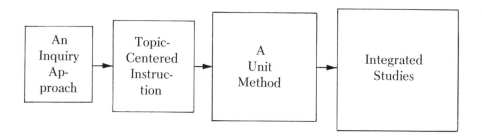

An Inquiry Approach to Learning

Those teachers who have restricted their classroom activities to lectures, reading the basic text, or assign-study-discuss procedures may find that an inquiry approach to learning is a first step in breaking away from the traditional, textbook-centered curriculum. In a simple inquiry approach the teacher poses challenging questions to lead to divergent thinking. For example, in considering a chapter heading in the textbook the teacher might ask the students to anticipate the author's organization of the topic under such a title. The ensuing class discussion might evoke questions and, as answers are sought, the text can be used as one source of information, but it need not be read page by page from beginning to end. In seeking answers to their questions the students will be consulting the index, practicing skimming, and using other reading skills. Thus a functional development of study skills is possible with a flexible use of the textbook.

A more advanced inquiry approach might be to utilize open-ended questions about problems in the local community: Why are few people shopping in the central business district? What can the owners of shops do to make the area more attractive? What kinds of shops and services are needed? In another situation, questions may result from direct experiences of children. Perhaps youngsters have accompanied their teacher on a walk around the school grounds looking for textures. Discussion may be stimulated by such questions as: Where are textures found? What makes textures different? How do textures affect our everyday living? The search for answers to these questions will draw upon subject content from many fields, will stimulate perceptual awareness, and will encourage students to improve their work and study skills. The spontaneous questions that children have about their environment also should be recognized and valued. If they bring materials into the classroom or if they raise questions about current news items, these too can be used as the basis for study.

With an inquiry approach the teacher must practice the art of asking open-ended questions rather than the type designed to elicit expected answers as in the Socratic method. Good questions from the teacher will prompt students to raise their own questions. As a matter of fact, the approach is most satisfactory when the questions originate with the children. Provisions for inquiry should lead to the consideration of meaningful problems for which answers have not been predetermined.

In summary, an inquiry approach is basically an open-ended question approach, centering around a problem about which students are encouraged to do divergent thinking. Some follow-up in depth should be stimulated. The activity may require only a short period of time, either in a classroom or on a field trip. Because an inquiry approach does not necessitate an elaborate structure, it can be implemented within the traditional classroom program.

Topic-Centered Instruction

A further step toward an integrated curriculum is the use of a topic-centered approach. The topic which serves as the center or focus for learning activities might be a chapter heading, it might be a teacher-planned problem, or it might be a topic posed by the children.

Many current textbooks are organized around topics or centers of interest. For teachers who need to rely on a basal text, a recommended procedure is to use the book as a guide to be supplemented by other related materials. Students can be encouraged to research different aspects of the topic and to locate and read appropriate sections of the text as well as supplementary sources.

Topic-centered instruction is not limited to reading activities. In the beginning, ideas for other activities may come from suggestions found at the end of a textbook chapter or in the teacher's manual. School-developed guidelines may suggest activities which encourage teachers to use a multi-media approach and to include related subject areas. For example, literature and music activities may be possible with a social studies topic. Science experiments, panel discussions, and dramatizations may be used to incorporate concepts and skills from other disciplines.

A topic-centered approach is more advanced than an inquiry approach because children can seek information, become involved in large and small group discussions, and share findings with the class. Through discussions children become aware of different interpretations of the materials used and of the varied opinions of others in the group. They test values, develop attitudes and appreciations, and become more skilled in human interaction. An integral part of topic-centered instruction is the use of carefully selected community resources.

A Unit Method

A more completely integrated curriculum is created through the use of a unit method in which teachers and students work together to plan and develop the study from beginning to end. Criteria for the selection of appropriate units are established by teacher-pupil planning, probably at the beginning of the school year. These criteria are used in selecting the unit. The class then specifies the objectives for the study. Problems and questions raised by the students are organized to determine the scope of the unit. Both pupils and teachers become involved in compiling a bibliography of resources including realia, field trips, resource people, audio-visual aids, and printed materials. A plan of study is decided upon. As the plan develops, the pupils and teacher consider those parts of the study to be undertaken by individuals, teams, small groups, and the total class. A time schedule is developed and places for work are designated. The teacher and pupils evaluate their progress in relation to their objectives and revise the plan of work as needed.

With the unit method, the content is used as a tool for learning and not an end in itself. The particular content which forms the focus for the study is less important than the types of learning involved. Thus it is of little consequence whether the class studies the department store, the dairy, or the pharmacy. Relevant content serves as the instrument to develop work and study skills, attitudes and appreciations, and social relationships.

In summary, the unit method is characterized by the integration of subject matter; it combines content with skill development; it engages teachers and pupils in cooperative efforts; and it unites the school with the community.

Integrated Studies

In unit teaching, children do not work on the unit throughout the entire day—nor should they. If the remainder of the day's activities are related to or suggested by the unit, a fully integrated program may evolve. As the teacher and pupils become more skilled in planning, subject matter lines disappear and artificial time schedules are no longer required.

As the unit progresses, the teacher diagnoses learning difficulties that later become the focus for special attention. A teacher can observe whether each child is using skills in a functional setting and can discover whether undeveloped concepts or misconceptions exist. The student, too, may realize a need for skills as he proceeds with his activities, and provisions for developing these skills can be included in the ongoing plans.

An integrated curriculum is most likely to emerge if a teacher is working with a given group of pupils over an extended period of time. The blending of subject areas into a community-centered curriculum can best be achieved in a self-contained classroom, in a block-of-time schedule, or in a flexibly planned team approach to learning.

THE INSTRUCTIONAL DESIGN FOR UTILIZATION OF RESOURCES: PEOPLE, TIME, AND SPACE

The move toward using the community as a classroom demands ever-increasing contacts with resources beyond the school setting. An instructional design that makes wise use of people, time, and space is essential.

Staff Cooperation

Cooperation is needed among all members of the school staff who have some contribution to make to the integrated study. Paraprofessionals, aides, student teachers, and special resource teachers should have opportunities to work with the classroom teacher. Administrators and central staff personnel can serve in consultative roles.

A close relationship must be established with the staff from the instructional resource center. If the center includes work, craft, and special interest areas, the pupils and teachers of all classrooms can work together regardless of assigned teacher responsibility for a particular class.

Teachers may meet together on a short term basis to plan specific activities for a given group of youngsters. Cooperative planning may be necessary when hallway bulletin boards or work areas are to be shared. If appropriate for the pupils involved, two or three teachers may arrange a learning experience in the community.

Staff cooperation is important when special group activities are desired. For example, a resource person may be available to appear for an assembly program or an audio-visual presentation may be deemed worthwhile. Culminating activities also may be shared by two or more classes.

Team teaching that involves three or four teachers planning together over an extended period for a given group of children is a further example of cooperation among professional staff members. To be effective, the team must have a designated meeting place and planning time during the school day. If a chairman is elected on a rotating basis, it is anticipated that shared leadership and shared decision making will result.

The principal may serve as a resource person. He can be involved as another member of the team. He may even accompany some of the children on community trips. In whatever capacity he serves as a resource person, he should know about the goals to be accomplished and why his permission should be granted for the variety of activities essential to the unit.

Paraprofessionals, aides, and student teachers must be included in planning the activities, too. They should be actively involved in the learning experiences—not considered as extra adults to accompany children on a trip. Since individuals, teams, and small groups of children may have responsibility for various phases of the study that include the use of community resources, added benefits may be accrued if aides and student teachers accompany small groups as needed. If additional assistance is required, parents can serve in such roles, too.

Flexible Scheduling

Because of the variety of activities in any integrated study, a flexible time schedule is essential. Both long and short range planning are necessary, and the time schedule must be adapted to the needs and activities of the group.

Perhaps the self-contained classroom provides the greatest possibility for flexible scheduling. If a teacher is working with a group of students throughout the school day, time adjustments can easily be made to accommodate the needs of the pupils.

Another type of flexible scheduling is a block-of-time arrangement in which two or more consecutive periods are scheduled together. In the junior high school, one teacher may have the responsibility for a given group of students in the social studies-English area. Within the two-period time block, a community study could be carried out which would integrate these two subjects.

Ideally, consultants should be available on a flexible time basis. They should serve an integrated studies program as resources rather than as special lesson teachers. The music teacher, art consultant, and instructional materials director should be available as needed to work with teachers and pupils. In the community-centered curriculum, these consultants will be identified as team members who work cooperatively with the classroom teacher to diagnose needs and to plan learning activities.

Multi-Age Grouping

Members of a community are not grouped by age; therefore, the school setting is more realistic if it reflects multi-age interactions at least some of the time. Multi-age groupings which more nearly resemble the society outside the school will enable children to develop social awareness and social sensitivity.

To initiate multi-age grouping some arrangement might be made for older children to work with younger children. In some tutorial plans, a selected group of older children works with younger pupils on a one-to-one basis, often for special help or practice in areas of need. Another arrangement might be class-to-class associations between older and younger students for the benefit of both groups. For example, ten-year-olds and six-year-olds might be teamed to go out into the community for firsthand experiences related to the unit and then return to the classroom to write language-experience stories, with the older students serving as secretaries for the younger ones.

The teenage secretary and the young storyteller both gain feelings of self-worth and sensitivity to others as they practice communication skills.

A class in which two traditional grade levels are combined into a "split class" offers a form of multi-age grouping. In such case the teacher should take advantage of possibilities for inter-age activities. This can be accomplished through the use of a unit approach rather than adhering to the usual grade level curricula.

Some schools are deliberately implementing multi-age grouping. Children of three age levels are grouped together on a proportional basis. For example, a classroom might have ten five-year-olds, ten six-year-olds, and ten seven-year-olds. Each year the oldest group will go to another teacher and ten younger children will be added. Thus the teacher has each child over a period of three years and the children have associations with different aged classmates throughout the period. [1]

[1] Warren W. Hamilton describes this organizational plan in "Multigrade Grouping: With Emphasis on Differences," in *Toward Effective Grouping* (Washington, D.C.: Association for Childhood Education International, 1962), pp. 54-56.

Family or House Plan

Another organizational scheme that is a possibility in a community-centered curriculum is the family or house plan. This plan has been used more widely in the English primary schools than in the schools of this country. In the family or house plan the school is organized as a house. Children are assigned to one room or area which serves as a coordinating center or home base for a teacher and a given group of pupils. There is great flexibility within the building as children move from one area to another. They can work with other teachers and with children of all ages as needs and interests dictate.

New schools designed for implementing a house plan differ drastically from the conventional school. Instead of a series of boxed-in classrooms, the new building provides an open environment in which there are many interest centers and work areas.

The family or house plan has all the advantages of multi-age grouping and, in addition, provides a setting in which the staff and student body can use the entire school as an instructional resource center.

A COMMUNITY-CENTERED CURRICULUM

In this chapter, the community and school are described as laboratories for learning. Children interact with their environment in the classroom, the school, and the community. Through the use of an inquiry approach to learning, topic-centered instruction, and a unit method, the integrated curriculum evolves. The instructional design for utilization of resources includes staff cooperation, flexible scheduling, multi-age grouping, and a family or house plan. This approach provides for environmental study which has relevance for learners and results in a community-centered curriculum based upon local problems and concerns as they affect the lives of pupils.

CHAPTER III

**THE COMMUNITY-CENTERED CURRICULUM
IN OTHER COUNTRIES**

The Community-Centered Curriculum
In Other Countries

To gather information about community-centered curricula in other countries the authors visited schools and museums in selected European countries, with many of the visits centering in England where major changes are occurring in the primary schools at both the infant and junior levels. Observations in the schools and discussions with educators led to the conclusion that many common problems are shared by teachers in other countries. Some of these problems are motivating youngsters, providing for individualized learning, promoting the development of communication skills, and trying to serve large groups of children effectively. Teachers are striving to establish meaningful learning opportunities whether they work with pupils in the poorly equipped older buildings or in the newer physical facilities planned especially for flexible programs. Schools museum officers, knowledgeable about curriculum, are working with local educators to enrich classroom offerings. The use of museum services, environmental studies, integrated day, and cooperative efforts among teachers are features that characterize some of the primary schools in England. Many of these curriculum practices seem to have merit for the schools in this country which are moving toward a community-centered program. The authors' general impressions of the English schools visited and selected examples of promising curriculum practices there are presented in this chapter.

GENERAL IMPRESSIONS OF SCHOOL PROGRAMS VISITED

The one general impression gained from visiting educational programs in England is that many desirable practices *do* exist in the schools to stimulate interest, creativity, self-direction, and social responsibility of children. The traditional schoolroom in which children sit at desks and listen to the teacher talk *can* be supplanted by an action-centered curriculum without sacrificing organization and teacher guidance. This impression is supported by observations of (1) the involvement of the children, (2) the activities of the teachers, and (3) the arrangement of the physical setting.

Impressions of the Involvement of Children

The most important evidence about the successes of educational endeavors comes from the children themselves. The pupils offer many indications that programs are responsive to their needs.

1. Children seem wonderfully self-directed and are intent upon their purposes as they set about their tasks.

2. Children are pleasant and friendly to guests in their schools. They sometimes ask questions about the countries visitors represent and show keen interest in other young people and world events. At other times pupils are so involved in their projects that visitors go unnoticed.

3. Children are engaged in problem-solving activities.

4. Children are not using sets of textbooks. Instead they rely upon a variety of resources suited to their individual needs.

5. No classroom was observed in which all children engage in the *same* activity. Some youngsters pursue individual projects and others work in small groups.

6. Children carry out meaningful projects which involve critical selection and use of materials rather than the copying of information from an encyclopedia.

7. Children are encouraged to be creative. Very young children write lovely poetry and fairly lengthy stories about their experiences. Creative writing is encouraged for *all* age groups. In arts and craft activities, predetermined patterns are not used.

8. Children are encouraged to communicate with each other and with adults. Emphasis is upon expressing ideas clearly.

9. Cooperation rather than competition is stressed. Children cooperate and assist each other in project work, reading activities, and in problem-solving generally.

10. Children are engaged in studying their local environment and relating it to the national and international scenes. They venture from the known to the unknown.

Impressions of the Activities of Teachers

Purposeful involvement of children occurs when teachers are enthusiastic and give careful attention to planning and organizing a learning environment. The following observations describe the activities of teachers in the schools visited.

1. Teachers are friendly and cooperative. With visitors, they are eager to describe their programs and to discuss common problems. With each other, they share ideas and evaluate efforts.

2. Teachers have good working relationships in an open environment created by the headmaster.

3. Teachers' objectives are focused upon the development of concepts and values rather than the teaching of isolated facts.

4. Teachers are well-organized—a requisite for the informal, flexible programs they carry out.

5. Teachers help children to plan daily activities and to assume responsibility for their plans.

6. Teachers praise pupils and encourage creative efforts. Evaluation is positive and self-evaluation is emphasized.

7. Staff members stress the importance and value of heterogeneous groups. Some teachers are deliberately attempting to get a wide age range through the use of family grouping.

8. Teachers and children are in various stages of their movement toward a more flexible program. They are learning together the responsibilities that accompany freedom.

The Community is the Classroom

Impressions of the Physical Setting

The physical setting reflects the planning of the teachers and makes possible the active involvement of children. In old and new buildings, the following features are found.

1. Teachers, administrators, and youngsters are very conscious of beauty. Art and beauty centers are in school corridors and in all classrooms.

2. Many books are provided for children to read for pleasure and for information. The areas set aside for reading in classrooms and in corridors usually have carpets, shelves of books, good lighting, and comfortable chairs.

3. Teachers use space creatively. For example, long tables are placed in corridors for art projects. Book shelves are used as dividers in the classrooms.

4. Displaying some work of every child is given high priority, and much of the available wall space in corridors and classrooms is used for this purpose.

5. Each child has some storage space. Class materials and children's individual work are kept in labelled drawers or compartments. Children have free access to supplies.

6. Furniture is flexibly used. Rows of desks have been replaced by tables and chairs grouped in work centers and interest areas.

7. School museum services contribute to the enrichment of the physical environment for learning. Art objects are used in beauty centers and many classroom projects are enlivened by the use of models or displays supplied by the museum.

The successful involvement of children, the activities of dedicated teachers, and the flexible arrangement of facilities blend together to create an integrated program related to life outside the school. Each school staff has much autonomy to develop programs which are responsive to the needs of pupils and which make use of the resources found in the local environment.

MUSEUM SERVICES

Museum services enrich the curriculum in many of the schools abroad. In many English communities, close cooperation exists between museums and schools, to the extent that schools museum officers are appointed to coordinate the services provided. The impetus for creating this position may come from the local school authorities or the museum may be the originating force.

The schools museum officer is expected to establish and operate a service for the purpose of making museum materials more accessible to the schools. His responsibilities include:

1. classifying and circulating materials.

2. collecting and preparing exhibits, models, and displays.

3. encouraging school visits to the museum.

4. orienting teachers to the museum services.

5. providing in-service training for teachers in the creative use of materials.

6. carrying out field studies with children in the local environment.

7. assisting children on an individual or group basis.

To work so closely with schools, a schools museum officer must have a thorough understanding of curriculum, be knowledgeable about the museum and its services, know the local area, and enjoy working with children.

A museum officer who has these qualifications works with schools in a variety of ways. He may initiate a museum service through the lending of original works of art, reproductions, or realia to the schools. He may create models and exhibits for use in the schools or the museum, and he may have technicians on his staff to prepare these displays. As exhibits are developed and loan materials become available, a card file or catalog is prepared for the use of teachers and students. A plan for distributing materials must also be devised, and many of the museums maintain their own delivery and circulation systems.

Another task of a schools museum officer is to make the museum itself more responsive to the needs and interests of children so that they will be encouraged to visit the museum and to look upon it as a resource. An example of an exhibit especially prepared for children is found in the Torquay Museum of Natural History, Devon, England. Here the schools museum officer and his staff have prepared an exhibit on "The Story of the Devon River." Animal and plant life appear in natural context as the story of the river unfolds. In this manner, an ecological study is presented in case exhibits. These exhibits are more effective than the usual presentation of a number of specimens all looking somewhat alike.

Displays which can be felt, manipulated, and operated provide direct experience for youngsters. The Deutsches Museum in Munich, Germany, is almost completely a working museum. Students of all ages can be found singly, in teams, or in small groups all over the museum observing models in operation, pushing buttons to activate displays, and trying various pieces of apparatus. They learn about mining processes, hydraulic engineering, shipbuilding, musical instruments, telecommunications, and many other facets of past and present day life by means of simulated experiences.

Sometimes in England a museum is literally taken to the school through open-ended exhibits that lead children to explore their own surroundings. The museum in Torquay has an excellent collection of loan kits for schools. One kit on "Tracks and Signs" includes an exhibit of rabbit fur found on a barbed wire fence and a display of leaves with indications that leaf miners have been at work. Through a series of questions, children are encouraged to look for tracks and other signs of animal life in their own locale. An exhibit on making bark and leaf casts includes illustrations and directions so that children can make casts of their own specimens. Another set of exhibits has birds shown in their natural habitat along with a corresponding local map showing where the birds are found in the area. Examples of rocks, fossils, and sea life are similarly displayed. Dressed dolls, tools, and farm implements are examples of other types of materials available for the children to feel and use.

In addition to these displays related to the local environment, schools museum officers often work directly with schools to carry out field studies that encourage children to become more perceptive about their surroundings. In some areas nature trails have been established and in a coastal village fieldwork is frequently carried out along the seashore. Museum officers also are helping to enrich the study of history by encouraging children to look at local building materials and by assisting pupils in the exploration of historical sites.

Teachers and students who are oriented to the materials and services provided by the museums often call or write to seek help in the identification of some object or to raise questions to be answered. One teacher was working with a group of children to design bird cages patterned on the natural forms in shells. Technicians at the museum took x-rays of shells and prepared an exhibit to stimulate children in many types of creative activities in art and mathematics as well as science. Because of their research, the students were able to design the bird cages. Another group of children studying the school building was able to use the museum service to obtain the early floor plans. Copies of maps and research documents were made available through the museum so that children could work from primary sources. These examples serve to illustrate the many ways in which schools museum officers contribute to local environmental studies.

As people in the community become aware of the museum's services to the schools, they are sometimes helpful in making additions to the collections. For example, a woman doctor who dresses dolls as a hobby is making historical figures for the museum at Torquay, and a nature lover who heard about the services of the Bowes Museum donated his collection of bird models.

Schools in rural areas make use of another service that the museum has to offer. In isolated areas or in schools that have a limited budget, science equipment is made available on a loan basis and the museum provides a service similar to that of an instructional materials center in a larger school system.

In addition to making a wide variety of materials available, schools museum officers also work closely with teachers. Some orientation is provided to acquaint new teachers with the services, and museum officers frequently conduct workshops in the local areas to enable experienced teachers to gather information and share ideas with their colleagues. Lesson plans are not prepared for museum materials because the emphasis is upon helping children to become more perceptive about their environment and to use the museum's resources in solving their problems. The workshops, therefore, are aimed toward helping teachers use the services flexibly and creatively.

ENVIRONMENTAL STUDIES

Having avoided the tyranny of textbook teaching, some teachers in England are using the natural interests of children and resources that are readily available in their area for environmental studies. Each locality has different resources, and the pupils and teacher in each classroom also have varying backgrounds and interests. It is not surprising, therefore, that the environmental studies which result are of many different types and are built around a wide range of themes with local and world-wide implications.

The very simple theme of "hands" was used by a primary teacher and her pupils to enrich vocabulary and to develop concepts. Some of the children were outlining their hands on paper when the alert teacher made use of this interest to introduce the term and concept of "silhouette." She also related the interest in hands to an earlier study of measurement by encouraging the children to measure and compare their hand spans and finger lengths. A discussion of the meaning of the term "hands" followed. The children mentioned the hands of a clock, which led to a further study of measurement as it relates to time. A feeling box was supplied so that pupils could touch different objects and textures and describe their sensations in as many different terms as possible. Thus an awareness of the sense of touch was combined with an activity to enrich vocabulary. This teacher had previously developed a flow chart in anticipation of some of the directions into which a study of hands might lead. She wanted to be able to capitalize on the children's suggestions, but she was wise enough to recognize that she could not predict all the ideas the youngsters would have about the topic.

Another teacher was helping a group of older children increase their sensitivity to color and its effects in the world around them. Language

A creative teacher and imaginative youngsters can plan many interesting learning activities by considering the question "What can we do with our hands?"

arts, science, fine arts, and mathematics were some of the areas that were incorporated into the study. The children were having creative experiences as they used colors in the development of geometric designs. Floral exhibits were prepared as a result of looking at colors and designs in nature. The unit focused on the importance of color in the natural world and the significance of color in modern society. Two examples of subproblems were the effects of color on plant propagation and the uses of color in advertising. Throughout the unit the children were given many opportunities to write creatively about color in their environment and about their emotional reactions to color.

Artistic arrangements are found in the classrooms and corridors of many of the schools. Collections of paintings, pottery, and textiles developed around a particular color are openly displayed so that children can see and feel. Flowers are in bouquets throughout the schools. The museum services cooperate with the schools in making the art objects available. In this manner, entire schools engage in environmental studies of color.

Many environmental studies are introduced through surveys of the local area. In one classroom later elementary children were writing about the development of their city. They constructed maps, drawings, and models and operated an information center to orient visitors to their area. Visitors could gain much information from viewing the projects and talking with the children who were eager to be helpful and to share their knowledge. One facet of their environmental study included a survey of the water services in the community. The city is a leading seaport and has a floating harbor, therefore water has played an important part in its development. The children had traced the water supply through the local rivers and dams, discussed the origin of the Plimsoll line, made trips to the harbor, and carried out a historical study by researching old Roman baths in the area.

A junior school, located in a lovely setting with a brook flowing through the grounds, has a small houseboat anchored at a "dock." Classrooms open on a play area and children are free to move in and out as needs arise. A part of the play area is reserved for gardening, and the children develop vegetable gardens and flower beds. One classroom carried out an environmental study that was initiated by an investigation of the rocks and stones in the area. Another class became interested in the stained glass windows of a nearby church and this interest led to related studies of colored glass, bottle designs and uses, prisms, and elementary principles of light rays.

The science center in the classroom supplements, but does not supplant, explorations of the natural environment. The tastefully arranged display serves as a beauty spot, as a room divider, and as an inspiration for questions and related investigations. Note the small storage drawers for children's materials.

In an older building housing upper elementary children, the entire school was engaged in environmental studies. Each class selected a different theme. One group developed a unit on animal life in the area. Another class was working on local architectural styles and became particularly interested in the terraced houses nearby. The teacher, whose hobby was photography, helped the youngsters make photographs of different types of architecture for use in the classroom. In still another class, the students were studying newspapers, journalism, and propaganda, and were creating their own class newspaper. All rooms in this school were engaged in project work, with the youngsters *actively* involved. The teachers served as resources and assisted with organizational plans. The children's development of responsibility and self-direction were clearly evident. Every teacher could leave his group to explain the unit to visitors while the children continued to work independently.

Although the curriculum is not planned around separate subjects, the use of the environment involves all of the traditional areas of knowledge. The point of start for any given study is not significant because any environmental topic invariably leads to the integration of content from many disciplines. One teacher, for example, was developing math concepts through the use of objects in nature. Using points in a circle, he was helping children develop patterns and shapes based on the arrangement of seeds in a pine cone and petals in flowers.

In another school, a class was carrying out a nature study project with the cooperation of some members of the community. One citizen provided the money to purchase seeds, plants, and shrubs for the village flower beds. A local gardener was serving as a resource person and the youngsters were providing a community service by spending some time each week on this project—their attempt to create some beauty in their town.

These examples are only a few of the environmental studies that were observed. Each unit or project was based upon the resources in the local area. Teachers can work with children of all ages in any community to launch similar studies by looking at their environment and raising questions about the normal activities around them.

INTEGRATED DAY

Project work creates a need for the flexible use of time, space, and materials. Project work also creates a need for integration of content areas. In many of the schools visited, teachers meet these needs through the use of the integrated day. Rigid time blocks disappear, to be replaced by a flexible time schedule in which teachers and pupils are free to plan learning activities around a theme and in terms of youngsters' academic needs.

Regardless of the time of day visitors enter the building, many children can be found working individually or in small groups on their projects or interests. In some cases a group of children can be found planning and evaluating with the teacher. Activities arise as a natural outcome of daily and long-range planning of individuals and groups. The teacher plans with the individual child so that both know the various activities to be carried out during the day. Each child, in turn, plans his own integrated day according to his needs and the availability of work areas and materials.

Teachers who work in an integrated day stress the importance of the "extended classroom" which provides space for noisy work, craft activities, and projects to "spill over" into adjoining rooms, corridors, or the out-of-doors. In schools designed for the integrated day, three or four classrooms are grouped around a central open area where large group activities, dramatic play, and construction work are carried out. If classrooms have doors leading into the play area, children are able to move in and out according to their work needs. In some schools garden plots are built into the play area and children work on gardening projects. One classroom had spilled over into the out-of-doors where several boys were dramatizing life on their improvised submarine. Many teachers and headmasters in older buildings are ingeniously devising means for more flexible use of space. Classrooms are extended into the long corridors which are used for project work, reading areas, and art activities. In one building an entrance hall, the only available space, is being used as a library and is staffed by the students. In these schools, there is nothing sacred about closed four-walled classrooms and corridors used only for passing.

Construction and painting activities "spill over" into the hall.

Boys are free to talk together, share ideas, and help one another with spelling as they compose their individual stories. The attractive display of paintings shows that children's work is appreciated.

Whether in old or new buildings, each classroom has a quiet spot, usually carpeted and quite tastefully decorated, where children go to read or work alone. Each room also has a center for the development of the concepts of math, at least one specially designated beauty spot, and much space devoted to the display of work created by the youngsters.

In these buildings, the teachers who utilize a topical or unit approach, with activities organized around interest areas and work centers, engage in much pre-planning. Most teachers develop work cards designating tasks of increasing difficulty planned to meet the needs of individual children in the room. Some of these tasks are simple projects to be completed and others are of the questions-for-study type. Frequently the cards have open-ended ideas, perhaps with a picture to stimulate creative writing or, in math, measurement activities may be suggested. These work cards, sorted according to subject area and difficulty, are filed in envelopes or packets in open areas of the room where children have ready access to them. When a child completes the tasks or projects on a particular card, he returns the card to the file and then moves to a new interest or takes another work card. As children gain experience with the integrated day, they become self-directed and can group themselves quite satisfactorily in the interest and work centers. They have the freedom to move into noisy or quiet areas as the need arises.

The long-range planning in which teachers engage is readily apparent in the flow charts they design around a theme and in the evaluation they plan for their programs. Through the use of the flow chart, the teacher attempts to predict the ideas and ensuing activities which may come from the introduction of a topic. A flow chart is not intended to be prescriptive of the scope and sequence of the study, but to serve as an aid to the teacher in organizing the learning environment.

Evaluation activities are planned to involve the students in self-assessment and are continuous from the beginning of the study. A type of open-ended evaluation form is often used which allows the student to evaluate himself in terms of his work schedule and individual program. He confers regularly with the teacher concerning the evaluation of his daily and weekly activities as well as his long-term goals. This type of evaluation replaces letter grades.

The flow of life in a classroom during an integrated day is similar to the flow of life in the world outside the classroom. In both situations, individuals organize their daily activities around the tasks they need to accomplish and the interests they wish to pursue.

COOPERATIVE EFFORTS AMONG TEACHERS

As teachers plan their programs around an integrated day, they find the sharing of ideas beneficial. In England teachers have many opportunities to plan together. Because of the extended classroom, the tea break, and talks around the lunch table, they have frequent informal contacts with one another. Furthermore, in some schools teachers have encouragement from headmasters and primary school inspectors to work together more closely.

Teachers in one school consider "cooperative teaching" a transitional step between the informal sharing of ideas and the more structured team teaching arrangements. Two teachers who indicated they are doing cooperative planning use a common work area where pupils' construction and cooking projects are carried out. The teachers plan activities for the area and encourage children from their rooms to participate on a self-selection basis. From this beginning these teachers hope to establish other shared interest and work centers so that children can move from one center to another and have the assistance of both teachers.

In contrast to the cooperative teaching which is evolving through informal associations, other teachers purposely plan together from the beginning of the school year. One group of four teachers, with a suite of rooms and a common work area, organized several interest centers. Each child is expected to do some work each day in the four areas of reading and writing, math and science, arts and crafts, and project work. Each child has a weekly plan of work and checks off activities as they are completed. Work cards are provided for many of the content areas, including some for their current study projects on transportation and electricity. This is an example of a planned type of team teaching.

Thus, cooperative efforts among teachers may range from informal daily contacts with colleagues to cooperative teaching as teachers feel confident and then to more formally organized team teaching.

IMPLICATIONS FOR AMERICAN SCHOOLS

Many desirable instructional practices in schools abroad can serve as inspirations for changes in this country. In this chapter, museum services, environmental studies, integrated day, and cooperative efforts among teachers have been suggested as desirable practices in a community-centered curriculum. Museums and historical sites can be used to much greater advantage than at present if the resources of these centers are available for children to observe and explore. Schools museum officers are needed to coordinate museum services with school programs. The local environment can offer rich resources in a problems approach to learning, and the integrated day can bring unity and coherence to school programs that have for too many years been compartmentalized by rigid time schedules and arbitrary divisions of subject content. Within the integrated day, teachers and students can plan individualized programs that have balance and continuity for the learners. As plans are implemented, the extended or open classroom can provide a setting for a variety of learning activities. Cooperative efforts among teachers can enrich the educational offerings available to students, and learners will have additional resources available to them in terms of professional personnel, space, and materials. Teachers, too, will find the sharing of ideas beneficial as they explore the possibilities of environmental studies carried out within the framework of the integrated day.

CHAPTER IV

INTRODUCING A COMMUNITY-CENTERED CURRICULUM

Introducing A Community-Centered Curriculum

A community-centered program seems to offer one of the most promising solutions to current problems in education. Visits to schools in other countries have shown that the community can be used effectively as a center for learning. In this chapter general objectives for a community-centered curriculum are set forth and suggestions are offered for initiating a program.

OBJECTIVES FOR A COMMUNITY-CENTERED CURRICULUM

A community school provides a realistic setting designed for pupils to:

1. raise significant questions from their experiences.

2. expand these questions into problems for study.

Work and
Study Skills

3. use multiple resources and techniques in solving problems.

4. work in meaningful relationships with others in problem-solving situations.

5. participate in planning learning experiences related to community life.

57

6. test values and resolve value conflicts.

7. develop social sensitivity.

8. increase perceptual awareness.

9. express themselves clearly and creatively.

Self-
Fulfillment

10. assume responsibility and become self-directive.

11. interact meaningfully with those of other social groups.

12. become aware of individual strengths and weaknesses.

13. participate as citizens in a democratic society.

14. understand the community as a related whole with its various sub-systems.

15. understand the world community concept.

Social Under-
standings

16. understand the natural, man-made, and human environments.

17. engage in community action and social service projects.

18. appreciate the cultural contributions of the community.

A program built around these objectives obviously will encompass more than traditional subject content, rigid time segments, and teacher-directed lessons. A few of the stated objectives can be accomplished through some of the field experiences commonly provided by schools; however, an effective community-centered curriculum requires a completely new approach, one which emphasizes work and study skills, self-fulfillment, and social understandings, and one which increasingly uses the community as a learning laboratory. Teachers and pupils who have followed a traditional curriculum may wish to move gradually into a community-centered program, perhaps by starting with an orientation unit.

USING AN ORIENTATION UNIT

At the beginning of the school year an orientation unit may be used to introduce the classroom, school, and local communities and to help teachers diagnose children's needs and interests in relation to the stated objectives. Children need introductory activities which will acquaint them with the program. Teachers, in turn, need to become acquainted with the pupil's skill development, experiential background, and individual interests and concerns.

An orientation unit can contribute to the development of rapport between the teacher and pupils as good working relationships are established. Pupils must become involved in the planning and they should share in the decision-making. Behavioral patterns for working together throughout the year are established in the first few weeks. Pupils need to develop skills of group work and independent study. They should engage in learning activities that require pre-planning and that take them away from the classroom, first on short excursions in the school building and later, as ground rules are established, on trips into the local community. In these activities the teacher is a facilitator, a resource, and, perhaps most important of all, the *adult* in the group.

The get-acquainted activities may start with simple discussions in the classroom. Children could respond to such questions as: How much do we know about our classmates? Their families? Hobbies? Likes and dislikes? Open-ended questions such as these lead to the development of language and social skills and help pupils develop sensitivity to the similarities and differences among people.

What do the children know about their own school? Do they know other teachers? Other students? The responsibilities of the principal? The school nurse? How many people are involved in keeping the school in operation? From a discussion of such questions, pupils may move to an exploration of the local community. What are the occupations of people in this community? Is this a complete community? Are there services or products essential to the community which are not available locally?

During these discussions teachers are diagnosing pupils' skills and assessing their knowledge. It is important that teachers do not resolve issues or answer all questions that the pupils raise. If youngsters do not understand the role of the corner store in the neighborhood, that is their question to answer, their problem to solve. Teachers need not feel the obligation to supply all the answers or to clarify all the misconceptions that are revealed. Instead they should help youngsters inquire and discover their own answers. While the students are finding and verifying information, the teacher is able to diagnose their learning-how-to-learn skills.

As the initial activities are carried out, skills of group work will be developed and ground rules for learning activities will be established. An introductory activity might consist of a visit to the school principal to interview him about his responsibilities in the school. Pre-planning of questions and interview procedures will be necessary and then, following the activity, an evaluation will be carried out by the class. Later a city official or businessman may be interviewed using many of the same procedures. The important point is that pupils are acquiring some skills of group work, interviewing techniques, and feelings of accomplishment from participating in a worthwhile learning activity. They are learning to work with a purpose in mind and, later, to evaluate in terms of that purpose. Furthermore, parents' understanding of the program is likely to be assured since the pupils will have purpose and a feeling of accomplishment and will convey their satisfaction to parents.

As pupils engage in a variety of introductory learning activities, the teacher notes misconceptions and assesses the topics which elicit the most response. Strengths and weaknesses in skill development are discovered along with areas of interest which the pupils wish to pursue further.

PROVIDING FOR COMMUNITY EXPERIENCES

In the orientation activities teachers become acquainted with pupils and their interests. Skills of working together are developed. Perhaps some further exploration into the community will follow. Helping children perceive their own natural environment will lead to many new experiences because children will begin to ask questions about familiar objects and events they have not been permitted to discuss in school previously. They will also ask questions about new discoveries they are making in their environment.[1]

Many short walks can be taken for specific purposes. Dorris Lee and R. Van Allen suggest that walks taken in the immediate vicinity of the school can help children perceive more carefully. Their perceptions become a means for expanding their concepts and enlarging their vocabularies

---

[1] Bill Martin, Jr. describes how an ant hill can be the inspiration for some interesting insights in *The Human Connection* (Washington, D. C.: Department of Elementary-Kindergarten-Nursery Education of the National Education Association, 1967).

and language patterns.[2] Some walks might be taken for the purpose of looking for shapes, colors, movements, and materials. Older groups can trace power lines, observe architectural designs, and identify local community problems.

Any of these activities can lead to the creation of stories, journals, books, or magazines. Relevant experiences and the language of the children are used to promote a wide variety of communication skills as well as to interrelate the traditional content areas of the curriculum.

BROADENING THE "COMMUNITY HELPERS" CONCEPT

Some of the activities commonly carried out to help children become aware of their own communities are the "community helpers" units. In the early grades the traditional community helpers units focus upon a limited number of occupations which are usually the most spectacular. Among these occupations are those of the policeman and the fireman. Equally important services of the gasoline station attendant and department store clerk are not investigated and often a broad perspective about the roles of the people of the community and their interrelationships is not created. For example, many young children do not realize that the policeman also may be a father, a ball player, a yard-raker—another human being. In Carl Roger's terms, the pupils do not view him as a "real person."[3]

Older pupils, who have become more aware of their own local community and who should become more deeply involved in local problems, are usually forced to study Ancient Greece or some other topic far removed from the contemporary scene. While some of these topics may have merit if approached in a meaningful way, they do not ordinarily contribute to pupils' understandings of today's society when they are studied in isolation. Therefore, it is more appropriate for these older students to expand the community helpers concept as they look at a wide range of community roles and investigate community problems.

[2] Dorris M. Lee and R. V. Allen, *Learning to Read Through Experience*, Second edition (New York: Appleton-Century-Crofts, 1963).

[3] Carl R. Rogers, "The Interpersonal Relationships in the Facilitation of Learning," in *Humanizing Education: The Person in the Process* (Washington, D.C.: Association for Supervision and Curriculum Development, 1967), pp. 1-18.

Problems that pupils identify for study should be those which are apparent at the local level. For example, in some of their exploratory activities older students may have identified architectural styles. If questions have been raised about the age of the buildings and the growth of the community, a study of urban development might naturally result. In a rural community students may have investigated the distance between homes. This might lead to a study of communication and transportation difficulties in a sparsely populated area. An investigation of local pollution problems may serve as an example of a conservation study which has nation-wide implications.

PROMOTING MULTI-CULTURAL UNDERSTANDING AND AESTHETIC VALUES

The emphasis in this book is on the development and implementation of a program of study based on the idea of the expanding community which includes the local, regional, and world communities. Today's space-age boys and girls, living in a one-world community, must have an appreciation for the different ways of living and the values held by other people everywhere. Harold Taylor stresses that the school has a responsibility to help youths develop such concepts and appreciations:

> *The conception of education itself must now be one which locates man intellectually in a universe described by scientists, artists, and writers, and in a cultural setting as big as the globe. To enjoy any longer the luxury of defining one's nation, one's society, or oneself in terms of pride of ancestry, social superiority, or power of destruction is not only supremely dangerous to the survival of the race, but intellectually and socially obsolete.* [4]

If schools are to commit themselves to fulfilling this responsibility, they face a tremendous challenge, and drastic curriculum changes must be made as soon as possible. One of the steps that can be taken immediately is to broaden the base of existing exchange programs. The most common type of program, the exchange of letters with children of other areas, can be expanded by the interchange of tapes, drawings, photographs, and realia. This will make some contribution to the promotion of cultural understandings and aesthetic values, but even more direct contact is needed.

---

[4] Harold Taylor, *The World as Teacher* (Garden City, New York: Doubleday and Company, Inc., 1969), p. 3.

Firsthand experiences can be obtained through exchange visits with other schools. Programs can be developed between suburban schools and inner-city schools so that inner-city children can participate in suburban activities and suburban children can become acquainted with inner-city problems. These visits are more effective when planned around specific objectives and when they involve the two groups of students in joint activities carried out over a period of time. Such programs are sometimes difficult to implement because of parental prejudices, which again indicates the need to increase human understandings because today's children are tomorrow's parents.

A rather common practice now is for older students to participate in exchange programs abroad. More adolescents should be afforded these experiences as an integral part of their studies rather than as a glorified trip. Even though a school has only one exchange student, countless benefits can be obtained if opportunities for association and sharing of information are wisely used.

To increase understandings in this country, teachers should take advantage of the possibilities existing in classrooms in which various ethnic backgrounds are represented. For example, Spanish-speaking migrants have had unique experiences which, if valued and shared, can make the curriculum more meaningful for them and more enriched for their classmates. Exchange programs may be carried out with Indian schools as another possibility. Also, children who have traveled can be encouraged to share their ideas.

Resource people in the community can be valuable in promoting multicultural understandings and aesthetic values. It is easy for teachers to overlook the wealth of resources in the local area. Often the least sophisticated person in the most unsophisticated community has much to offer. Enoka H. Rukare points out that a professional hang-up with African educators is that they may believe that the illiterate African has nothing to offer, whereas in reality many of the people actually represent "mines of African wisdom." [5] He then cites the example of ". . . an old woman in South Uganda who knows the names and classes of nearly every plant and grass in the region and who is believed to be the private family medicine adviser to

---

[5] Enoka H. Rukare, "Aspirations for Education in the 'New' and Free Nations of Africa," *Educational Leadership* 27 (November, 1969), p. 127.

a number of the African medical doctors at the neighboring government hospitals."[6] Surely there are many such untapped resources in every local community.

Further understandings can be promoted through a closer look at the local customs and values. For example, within the community families follow different customs in holiday observances. Through a study of the observance of Thanksgiving, pupils can look at various customs people have developed centering around the holiday. The origins of the customs can be traced and the reasons for the many variations can be discovered. While schools are not permitted to teach religion, they can teach *about* religions. Studying the religious institutions in a local community will help pupils to understand many of the similarities and differences that exist among religious groups.

In chapter three, various types of museum programs have been described and services provided to schools by museums have been outlined. Such facilities offer a treasure-trove of opportunities for interesting learning activities based upon concrete experiences. A one-shot excursion to the local historical museum does not, however, illustrate wise use of that resource. Rather, pre-planning carried out between teachers, pupils, and the museum staff is necessary so that each visit will grow out of the needs pupils have identified and will become an integral part of the total learning experience.

Children should understand that aesthetic values change over periods of time. Perhaps on a short walk from school they will observe that Victorian architecture, which seems characterized by so much gingerbread today, must have been valued at an earlier time in history. A study of architectural styles might lead into a consideration of related changes in music, dress, and even automobile design. Countless possibilities exist for developing aesthetic values through an integrated approach.

The importance of tradition in perpetuating the culture is exemplified by folklore. Because of its appeal to children, folk literature might be used to help pupils realize the universal interest in stories and songs and become aware of the common themes found throughout the world.

[6] *Ibid.*

Taylor reminds us that:

> . . . *it is necessary to understand modern man as a single member of the human race with infinite individual variations, and not as the representative of a single culture, nation, society, or continent.* [7]

STIMULATING AWARENESS OF THE EXPANDING COMMUNITY

Awareness of the expanding community is stimulated through the implementation of a community-centered program which has as its objective an integrated curriculum, integrated between the school and community as well as within the traditional content areas. In developing such a program, the orientation unit would only be an initial step in helping children understand the school setting and the local community. The ideas of the expanding community that children bring to school as they share personal travel experiences, television programs, and discussions of space exploration can be used to enrich the classroom program. Firsthand community experiences can be provided to help children acquire language and perceptual skills and to stimulate an awareness of the expanding community. Broadening the community helpers concept through a study of current problems such as urban development and pollution is much to be preferred over the usual attempts to motivate children through artificial means. In this chapter, suggestions have been offered for bringing into existence an integrated curriculum in a community-school setting.

[7] Harold Taylor, *Loc. cit.*

CHAPTER V

**COOPERATIVE PLANNING
AND
A PROBLEMS APPROACH IN
A COMMUNITY-CENTERED CURRICULUM**

Cooperative Planning And A Problems
Approach In A Community-Centered Curriculum

The implementation of the integrated curriculum in the community-school setting requires cooperative planning. Special teachers must cooperate with regular classroom teachers; subject area teachers must work together in order to break the traditional subject barriers. Teachers unaccustomed to the unit or problems approach may receive stimulation and security from planning and working together. Supervisors and administrators must be knowledgeable about the program in order to facilitate and support teachers' efforts. In all cases, the people involved must be aware that an integrated curriculum demands cooperative effort, the use of multi-media, and a wide range of activities appropriate to the objectives. Teachers will need time to develop the necessary skills for involving pupils in cooperative planning experiences, and they also will need to gain confidence in sharing ideas about curriculum planning. In this chapter some suggestions will be made for teachers to move into cooperative planning and to use a problems approach for implementing a community-centered curriculum.

MOVING AWAY FROM THE BASIC TEXT

Perhaps teachers will first wish to move away from the basic text through the use of a multi-media approach. As they feel comfortable and secure in doing so, they may bring additional books and audio-visual materials into the classroom. They will want to involve pupils in the search for materials. Teachers and pupils may look for related materials in the school's instructional resource center, and pupils may be encouraged to bring in additional materials from their homes and to suggest resource people from the community for possible contributions to the study. Through these efforts pupils and members of the community become involved in cooperative planning, albeit on a rather structured basis at this stage.

Many teachers are already providing additional materials in their classrooms, but they sometimes fail to recognize that a multi-media approach, to be effective, also requires a wide variety of activities. For example, the teacher who makes use of a supplementary set of texts can divide the class into two groups with each group using a different reference to seek information about the topic under study, followed by a discussion in which the ideas from the two resources can be compared. A better approach would be to have the children raise some questions about the topic and then use their references to find answers to the questions. Findings need not be limited to two references; teachers and pupils will quickly discover that they also may use filmstrips, resource people, and exhibits to add to their information. Instead of having feedback to the class in the form of discussions or reports, pupils will be encouraged to be creative in their use of demonstrations, art work, and dramatizations.

TEACHERS PLAN TOGETHER

If provisions are made for teachers to have released time for in-service activities to plan a community-centered curriculum, they can begin to work together and share ideas for using a variety of materials and resources. They can discuss activities in which pupils can become involved. A discussion of the various uses of role playing might bring new meaning about a technique that has been known in name only to some teachers. Such shared experiences are the first steps in creating a rich "bank" of ideas for the development of a resource unit from which teachers can draw suggestions for objectives, activities, and materials.

Time for planning might be provided at the beginning of the school year, as in a two-week workshop. Some schools provide half-day work sessions throughout the year. Colleges and universities should be encouraged to work with the local schools in helping teachers plan resource units, become familiar with the community, and develop skills to implement unit teaching. (This keeps a college staff in touch with reality.) Special teachers in the schools should also be involved in the planning sessions, thus increasing the possibility of an integration of subject areas into a more meaningful whole. Pre-student teachers, student teachers, and interns who are working in the school should be involved too.

DEVELOPING A RESOURCE UNIT

Meaning of the Term "Resource Unit"

A resource unit is a storage bank of suggestions for objectives, content, activities, evaluation, and materials on a given theme or problem. It serves as a guide for teachers as they develop teaching units with their pupils in the classroom. Ideally a resource unit should be compiled through the efforts of teachers cooperating in the sharing of their unique talents and experiences. Such sharing is particularly important for teachers working in a community-centered curriculum. They can contribute their perceptions and understandings of the local community and undoubtedly this interaction will foster their effectiveness in team teaching. Resource units may be planned by individuals but such materials do not represent the group thinking which goes into the preparation of units written by several teachers working together.

A resource unit is much more comprehensive than a teaching unit. It is deliberately planned so that many teaching units can evolve, each unit appropriate to the needs of a given group. Because a resource unit is broad in scope, teachers are encouraged to be creative and engage in teacher-pupil planning.

A resource unit should include: an introduction or overview; generalizations or concepts to be developed; objectives; scope or broad outline of content; suggested activities; resource persons and materials; and evaluation procedures. It may also include a vocabulary of terms.

A Form for a Resource Unit

Resource units may be organized in a variety of ways. A sample form is presented here. Some teachers may prefer a flexibly organized file or folder so that they can make revisions and additions more easily. Because the resource unit is suggestive and flexible, it should be designed so that it can be used creatively.

71

I. The Unit Title

The title should be stated as a problem; it must be definitive. It should stimulate the interest of the learners. For example, a title "How Did Our Community Develop?" is more meaningful than "Our Community."

II. Introduction

The introduction should include a very brief overview of the scope of the unit. For example, an introduction to the unit titled "How Did Our Community Develop?" might be:

This unit is designed to relate the real world in which children live to their learning activities in school. The intent is to help children become more aware of their own environment and realize how it has developed and changed. Emphasis is upon the people who have contributed to the local area and the children will have an opportunity to help the community become more aware of multi-cultural values. The interdependencies locally as well as in the expanding community will be studied. The unit draws content from geography, history, mathematics, science, sociology, anthropology, economics, political science, literature, art, and music; it incorporates functional language, reading, and study skills.

III. Generalizations

Statements of generalizations indicate that teachers have given thought to the basic understandings which pupils should derive as a result of their learning experiences. For example, generalizations that might be derived from the sample unit include:

A community is developed by many people who have common needs and who can make certain unique contributions.

Life in a community is related to environmental conditions and to the traditions of the people.

People in a community are interdependent and their interdependence extends beyond the boundaries of the local community.

A community is constantly changing.

IV. Objectives

Objectives stated for the unit should be limited to those to be advanced by that particular unit. They should be stated in behavioral terms if possible and should be categorized as understandings, skills, and attitudes. For example, in the unit on the community some of the objectives might be:

As a result of the experiences in this unit, pupils should be able to:

Work
and
Study
Skills

interview people.

compile charts and graphs.

compare and evaluate data from various sources.

Under-
stand-
ings

give reasons for the changes in the community.

explain how the community has developed and maintained its traditions.

describe the institutions and services found in the community.

Atti-
tudes

appreciate the contributions of many people to life in the community.

appreciate the memorials and historical sites as clues to the establishment and growth of the community.

expect and accept the variations of traditions within the community.

V. Scope

The scope of the resource unit includes the broad outline of the problem and of its sub-problems. Major topics should be developed sufficiently to indicate content that is related to purposes and is of significance to the pupils. For example, in the unit on the community, a *partial* list of problems might be:

A. How have the man-made features of our community developed?

   1. Houses

      a. What are the types and styles of houses?

      b. What do these houses reveal about the people who built them?

      c. How have the houses changed over time?

   2. Schools

      a. What are the different types of schools?

      b. How do our schools differ from the earlier ones?

   3. Industries

      a. What industries are located in the community?

      b. How did they get started?

      c. What others were here before these?

      d. How are the present ones like or different from earlier ones?

B. Who are the people in our community?

   1. Settlers

      a. Who were the first settlers?

      b. Why did they come?

      c. Where did they locate?

      d. What did they do?

   2. Population growth

      a. How has the population grown and changed over the years?

      b. What has caused these changes?

   3. Our families

      a. When did our own families arrive?

      b. Why did they come to this area?

4. Newcomers

    a. Who are the newcomers today?

    b. What countries do they represent?

    c. How can they help us increase our multi-cultural awareness?

VI. Activities

Learning activities should be varied and must be planned so that the objectives are carried out. They should be designed with the individual differences of pupils in mind and should give the students experiences in planning and working together. Many activities should be stated for every objective; more activities should be included in the resource unit than can be used in any one teaching unit.

Research activities provide essential background information. They can take the form of: reading in texts and other printed material; locating information on maps, charts, and graphs; interviewing and listening to people in the classroom, in the community, on radio and on television; viewing pictures, slides, moving pictures, and filmstrips; observing places, processes, and objects; experimenting with different ways of compiling and sharing information.

Creative activities not only show a child's interpretation of concepts basic to understandings but also give him personal satisfaction and encourage him to be resourceful. Creative activities may include: drawing and painting pictures, murals, and posters; modeling and constructing objects, projects, and dioramas; writing stories, plays, poems, and songs.

Other activities can provide for continuity and sharing. Pupils can keep records such as a daily class journal and can make experience charts or outlines that show the steps in planning. They can make graphs and other visual representations. Sharing in discussions and dramatizations are other possible activities.

In the unit on the community, some possible activities are:

Look at historical houses in the community. Compare the styles and materials with newer houses. Talk with the owners about the original buildings and their occupants.

Plot points of interest on local maps.

Use reference books to find out where and why the first settlers came.

Survey our own families to see how they happened to settle here.

Make an exhibit of the natural resources in the area.

Make a list of articles used in the community that come from other places — foods, clothing, gasoline, manufactured goods. Show on maps where they come from. Find out how they are obtained.

Make a list of items brought in to the community in earlier times.

Culminating activities are evaluative experiences that highlight the generalizations, concepts, and possible solutions to the problem that has been under study. These activities may take the form of demonstrations, exhibits, dramatizations, discussions, or other types of planned programs. The pupils must have an opportunity to summarize and assemble their findings into an integrated whole.

VII. Evaluation

Evaluation activities should be based upon the objectives for the unit and should be an integral part of all the learning experiences which are carried out. A wide variety of activities should enable both pupils and the teacher to evaluate individual and group effort and to acquire new learnings about themselves. Appropriate procedures should be included for each of the objectives stated, and formal and informal types of evaluation should be utilized.

Pupils can be guided to clarify goals, state problems, plan solutions, delegate responsibilities for carrying out plans, and evaluate progress. For example, note how a consideration of the following questions involves a relationship between goals and activities and yet the focus is on the evaluative process:

What are we trying to find out or do? Why is it important? How shall we do it?

What resources are available and how shall we use them?

Who will assume responsibility for each task?

How are we improving in our ability to work together?

How are we improving in reading, speaking, listening, and writing skills? Are we learning any new words?

What are we learning that we ought to remember?

What shall we do next?

VIII. Vocabulary

The vocabulary section should include a listing of terms appropriate to the unit which the students might be expected to meet during the study. These terms and concepts should be developed as an integral part of the unit and not as isolated vocabulary lessons. The list in the resource unit should include some notes about word derivations as well as ideas for stimulating interest in the vocabulary. For example, the term "community" stems from the word "common" and an awareness of this derivation could lead children to begin to see some relationships with "town commons," "commonwealth," "communion," "communicate," and "communism." The seemingly illogical spelling of "neighbor" might be more sensible to students if they are helped to see that the word can be traced back to its derivation from a combination of a word for "nigh" meaning "near" with a word "gebur" meaning "farmer." Pupils can also be encouraged to consider the changes in language meanings that occur as society changes—"neighbor" now has a much broader frame of reference than "nearby farmer" and the "commonness" has implications for the concept of a "world community."

IX. Resource Materials

A wide variety of materials should be included in the resource unit. The list should be specific and the materials should be readily available locally.

Teachers working cooperatively can develop a more extensive and varied listing of resources than one teacher working in isolation. A "Community-Classroom Workshop" provides the time, facilities, and consultants for groups of teachers to explore and evaluate local resources and to consider how these might be used in the instructional program.

If the form for the unit has been kept open, resources can be added as they are suggested through the teaching unit, and notes can be made as to the value of the resources used.

The resource unit should include the following types of materials:

A. Community resources
  1. Historical sites and monuments

  2. Museums, especially the living museums which preserve early life styles

  3. Businesses and industries, ranging from a one-man operation to a complex factory

  4. Institutions, including examples of a local unit's relationship to its national or international organization

  5. Resource people such as parents, senior citizens, teacher education students, and high school volunteers who can make individual contributions in the form of services, demonstrations, and shared experiences as in the following examples:

    a. Parents who can knit, operate a ham radio, show how an automobile engine works, or demonstrate any other activity of everyday community life

    b. Parents who can serve as paraprofessionals to assist teachers in their work with children in the classroom and the community

    c. Senior citizens who can describe early life in the community

    d. High school volunteers and senior citizens who can read to a child or accompany a small group into the community

  6. Community landmarks such as bridges, depots, and mills

  7. Commonly overlooked resources such as lampposts, fences, ant hills, and electric-eye doors

B. Audio-visual materials

  1. Films, filmstrips, and slides

  2. Maps, charts, murals, bulletin board displays, graphs

  3. Pictures and photographs

  4. Models, mock-ups

  5. Television and radio programs, tape recordings

C. Printed materials

    1. Books

        a. Textbooks

        b. Reference books

        c. Trade books and fiction

        d. Supplementary materials, including free materials distributed by Chambers of Commerce, businesses, and service organizations

    2. Periodicals, newspapers, pamphlets, brochures

    3. Documentary materials

The outline for a resource unit presented here can serve as a model for teachers who may wish to develop one for their own use. Some examples have been presented for each section of the outline. A resource unit is written by teachers and, as the name implies, is a resource or guide for planning a teaching unit with pupils.

A TEACHING UNIT EVOLVES

The teaching unit is not written. It evolves in the classroom as the teacher and pupils plan their activities together around a central theme or purpose. Such a unit cannot be imported by plans and activities imposed by the teacher, by the textbook, or by some commercially packaged product.

The length of the teaching unit varies with the age of the pupils, the particular focus of the experiences, and the depth to which the class feels a need to explore.

A good working relationship among the pupils and between the pupils and the teacher should have developed in the early orientation period. The children should have experienced a gradual introduction to the use of the classroom as a laboratory for learning and should be acquiring the skills that lead to responsible self-direction. The work centers and interest centers should have been established and, with the teacher's help, the children should be able to move from one center to another making use of the available resources as needs arise.

In this open setting which reveals children's concerns and perceptions, an alert teacher can help youngsters identify a major problem for study, one that is sufficiently broad in scope to satisfy a wide range of individual differences. Thus a teaching unit begins to evolve as the teacher engages the pupils in cooperative planning. If a resource unit is available on the topic, the teacher can draw upon it for additional suggestions and help. A more detailed description of the steps for implementing a teaching unit is presented in this section.

Establishing Criteria

During the orientation period, the students and teacher can establish some criteria for the selection of a problem for study. Although the criteria are cooperatively established, a list might include:

Will this study help us understand our own community and everyday living?

Will we gain an increased awareness of the world community?

Can we work toward some solution or partial solution to the problem?

Can we carry out a variety of activities that will meet a range of related interests and abilities?

Are sufficient materials and resources available?

Are a number of content areas included?

Are there opportunities for skill development?

Is the topic meaningful to us now and will it be useful to us in the future?

Selecting the Unit for Study

Problems for study may be selected in a number of ways. If the school has a study guide, resource units, or a listing of topics to be studied during the year, a selection may be made from that source. When the class has some freedom to select areas for study, and if the teacher is experienced in cooperative planning, problems can emerge through class discussions of community activities or of current events. Interests and concerns of students may suggest topics for study. In any case, from among the suggestions, the teacher and students try to reach a consensus about the selection of the problem. Their ideas are evaluated against the criteria established earlier. Some possible problems for local community study might be:

How have ethnic groups contributed to our community?

How is our town changing?

How can recreational facilities be improved in our community?

As the teacher becomes increasingly skilled in cooperative planning and in the use of the unit approach, he will feel secure in moving to a study of more controversial issues. Many problems that are interesting and important to students are of a controversial nature. Teachers and students should be encouraged to study about such topics as integration, religious institutions, student unrest, and military involvements in other countries.

If the teacher has had little experience with a unit approach to teaching and if there are predetermined topics for study, it is still possible to involve students in cooperative planning within the established framework. Teachers and pupils may develop the pre-planned topic around their own objectives. They are free to define the scope of their study, relate the topic to their experiences and the local community, plan a variety of activities, select materials, and plan for evaluation.

Formulating Objectives

When the problem has been selected and phrased as a question, teachers and pupils should work together to state the objectives. The objectives developed in the classroom as the teaching unit evolves will not be the same as those developed by the teachers who wrote the resource unit. As the teacher and the pupils plan objectives together, their suggestions are listed on the chalkboard or on an overhead projector, perhaps written by a student who serves as secretary for the group. When the students become more accustomed to stating objectives, they may be able to categorize them as understandings, skills, and attitudes and appreciations; however, in the beginning the group might not make such distinctions.

In listing the objectives students may be more likely to concentrate on behavioral growth if the objectives are prefaced with:

When we complete this study we should be able to . . .

The completion of that phrase will then indicate the behaviors they expect to develop. For example, when we complete this study we should be able to (a) be of service to the community and (b) help the community become aware of the contributions made by its citizens.

The Community is the Classroom

Planning the Study

After the objectives have been developed, the class will plan the scope of its unit. Suppose the group has decided to study the topic "How have regional and ethnic differences contributed to our community?" Some questions raised by youngsters might include:

What dialect and language differences are found in our community?

How have street names in our community originated?

What are some interesting hobbies or talents that people have brought to our community?

These and other questions pupils have raised about the topic can be listed and organized. With the teacher's guidance, the outline can be expanded to include further questions that will ensure more depth in the study.

A plan of work must be developed. In the beginning, the class may decide upon some exploratory activities such as: a general discussion, various types of background reading, talking with parents and grandparents, a planned trip into the community, or a search in the instructional materials center for appropriate resources. These initiating activities are planned cooperatively in relation to needs, goals, and materials, and they may take a variety of forms.

Carrying Out Unit Activities

As the unit progresses, the experiences of the group will lead to new experiences and new activities. For example, in the topic "How have regional and ethnic differences contributed to our community?" some activities might be:

Make a survey of community expressions that are regional in origin. For example, do you say bag, sack, or poke? Do you travel on a freeway, an expressway, or a thruway? Compile this information for the school newspaper, giving reasons for the different expressions.

Trace the origins of street names. Inquire from city officials as to how street names are assigned.

Collect information on interesting hobbies or talents in our community. Make use of small group interviews, first conducting some practice sessions with school personnel. Pupils take photographs, make recordings, or collect samples of hobbies or talents represented in the neighborhood.

Research the origins of special foods and recipes that are favorites in the community: pizza, chop suey, hamburg, chittlins, pasties. Prepare some of these foods in school, using mothers as resources and aides. Display pictures of foods or recipes and show their origins on a map.

Hopefully each student will participate in individual study, small group work, and some total group activity. Each pupil will also be involved in many learning experiences so that he becomes familiar with using a variety of resources and develops such skills as interviewing, participating in panel discussions, taking notes, outlining, reporting, and giving demonstrations.

In an open classroom with children engaged in the types of community-centered activities just described, the following scene might be observed by a visitor to the school:

In one area children are at a listening post to hear their taped interview with the custodian in order to evaluate their interviewing techniques.

Some children are making a pictorial record of regional words used for various objects or activities.

A child is at the chalkboard writing a story about the hobby of a family member. Another child is typing a story and one is proofreading with the help of another class member.

Two youngsters are using reference books to trace the origin of pasties.

A small group is in the cooking area making pasties with a mother's help.

Some children are using reference books to compile a list of services and goods needed in a community.

Two boys and a girl are looking through old magazines for pictures of essential community services.

Other children are engaged in various activities not related to the central theme but which are a part of the total balanced curriculum planned by the teacher and pupils. Measuring activities are underway in the math laboratory. Children are also observed reading in the library corner and some are in the corridor working on a painting project.

A culminating activity should summarize and tie the unit together. It should reflect the many different activities and experiences that have been a part of the unit. It might indicate some solutions to the problem under study. In some cases, the culmination of one unit will provide transition into another unit.

Culminating activities for the community study partially described in this section might consist of:

Creating a magazine or book about our neighborhood with copies to be distributed in the community.

Displaying charts, photographs, stories, and recipes in a local bank or business place. Children could make posters or write newspaper ads to stimulate local people to visit the display.

Preparing and presenting a program on a local television station, highlighting the diverse talents and special resources in the community and showing how these are a miniature representation of the expanding multi-cultural world in which we live.

In these three examples of culminating activities, the children are moving out into the community with the results of their study and the community becomes a classroom for all of its people.

Evaluating the Unit

Evaluation begins with the selection of the problem for study. As possible problems are measured against the criteria established by the class, initial evaluation is carried out. The framework for the ongoing evaluation is determined by the objectives. Each activity must be judged in terms of its contribution to the objectives, and since there are many types of objectives and activities, there should also be many types of evaluation. Both formal and informal measures should be used to evaluate individual and group efforts. For example, if the objective is that of being able to participate effectively in class discussion, one form of evaluation might be the use of participation charts made by the students. Such charts can be used for individual evaluation as well as for evaluating the discussion skills of the group. A few other forms of evaluation include observations, conferences, group discussions, summary charts, written projects, and rating scales. In the learning activities suggested as a part of the community study, children were engaged in evaluative activities as they listened to their recorded interview and as they proofread their story together.

A culminating activity can serve as a final evaluation. In any one of the three culminating activities—the creation of the magazine, the display in the local community, and the presentation of a television program—children can integrate their many learning experiences into a project that becomes a practical test of their accomplishments.

LIVING AND LEARNING TOGETHER

The cooperative planning that is a requisite for the development of a community-centered curriculum brings many people together to solve a common problem. As resource units are planned, classroom teachers, special teachers, administrators, and consultants begin to share ideas and gain deeper appreciations for the contributions each has to offer. They also come to a realization that their combined efforts can lead to a much stronger and more relevant curriculum for children than one which is put together piecemeal.

Teachers and pupils begin to communicate with one another as they become increasingly skilled in the problem-solving techniques that are inherent in the evolution of a teaching unit. Students begin to communicate with young people in other cultures as they engage in studies of the expanding community. They establish contacts that help them to understand the concept of the interrelatedness of all peoples. Through their experiences in the community-centered curriculum, students learn about life in the real world because they are living it.

CHAPTER VI

**A COMMUNITY-CENTERED CURRICULUM
IN ACTION**

A Community-Centered Curriculum
In Action

Thus far in the discussion of the learning environment for a community-centered curriculum, the assumption is that there has been a gradual progression from the traditional classroom structure to a more open and informal setting. The teacher has engaged in some pre-planning and has helped the pupils to use the available organized materials and resources within a framework that has been somewhat predetermined. During this period the teacher and children have acquired skills of working together in planning a topic for study that extends beyond the textbook approach and makes use of the resource unit. Furthermore, some of the usual topics such as housing facilities and contributions of ethnic groups have been approached through teacher-pupil planning and a variety of direct contacts in the community.

The purpose of this chapter is to describe a community-centered curriculum in action after a teacher has had considerable experience with cooperative planning and is sufficiently flexible to permit the theme for study to emerge from the interests that children have in the ordinary events that touch their lives. The spontaneously initiated theme is developed into an integrated unit as the teacher and pupils plan their activities together and become increasingly involved in the life of the community.

AN IDEA IS BORN

The coming of spring in Michigan is a dramatic event which is readily observable by children and adults alike. The warming sun gradually melts the snow, and while waiting for the ground to dry boys dig to the bottom of their "treasure boxes" to retrieve long-forgotten bags of marbles. Girls, too, are caught with enthusiasm as they come forth with jump-ropes and roller skates. Sometimes the changing of the seasons seems to occur so abruptly that children who have gone to school in winter's cold in the morning are alive with the feeling of spring when they return to school after lunch.

In an open classroom this bubbling excitement can be captured by a creative teacher who is sensitive to the spontaneous reactions of children. Because she is flexible, the teacher listens and encourages the youngsters to share their perceptions and to anticipate other events which will occur. In addition to the children's own rediscovered recreational activities, the discussion includes comments that snowmobiles will no longer be transported on the highways, heavy winter clothing can be stored away, and baseball teams will go into spring training. The teacher stimulates further discussion by means of her open-ended questions:

> What other changes have we seen?
> How does spring make us feel?
> How can we describe spring?

After some consideration of these questions and others like them, a suggestion is made that the change in seasons might be a worthwhile theme for study.

At first glance, such a topic may seem quite common and have little relationship to an in-depth community-centered study. However, careful thought will reveal that almost any theme has a wide range of possibilities for implementing a community-centered approach. The process of learning about life can occur with many themes, provided the emphasis is upon the approach rather than on the theme itself.

THE POSSIBILITIES ARE EXPLORED

The teacher begins to consider with the children the possibilities for learning opportunities centered around the coming of spring with all its broad ramifications. She asks, "If we are to study the effects of the coming of spring upon our community, what are some of the questions we shall want to answer?"

As in all classrooms, such a question elicits a random assortment of comments and suggestions. Some children have already been sparked by their own special and rather limited areas of interest to which they cling tenaciously, making it difficult for them to contribute to the total planning. A few children seem not entirely excited by the idea. Most, however, become engaged in offering questions and ideas for class consideration:

How does the coming of spring affect weather?
How does the change in weather affect people?
How does our community change in appearance?
Who pays to repair the chuckholes in our streets?
Where have flies, turtles, and butterflies been all winter?
Why do baseball teams have spring training?

The teacher as the adult group member builds upon these suggestions and asks further questions to help children become aware of broader and deeper aspects of the theme. The questions which emerge appear sufficiently promising to cause the class to evaluate the theme against the criteria for selecting a unit which they established earlier in the year.[1] Satisfied that the topic offers challenge and interest, the class selects the question "What Are the Effects of the Coming of Spring upon Our Community?" as the focus for study.

A SETTING IS CREATED

During the selection of the topic and in subsequent activities and planning, it is assumed that the teacher and pupils have progressed through the steps of a teaching unit outlined in Chapter V. This progression has occurred at intervals over a period of time and has led to the establishment of objectives, the identification of sub-problems, the definition of scope, the planning of activities, the consideration of national and international aspects of the study, and the use of community resources.

The study reaches a point at which children are completely involved in a rich learning environment centered in an open classroom but extending beyond into the school and the community. Work centers and areas of interest have been developed around the chosen theme; beauty centers expressing the spring motif are found in the classroom and corridor; and arts and crafts areas are designated for projects underway. Evidences of service projects

---

[1] An example of criteria for selecting a unit of work is presented on page 80.

will soon be apparent on the school grounds and in the community. This learning environment now provides an observer the opportunity to view a wide variety of related activities which blend together into an integrated curriculum giving children a feeling of unity as they work in diverse ways toward a common goal.

THE ACTION IS UNDERWAY

Stepping into the classroom which is the focal point for this study, one's first impression is that children are working together helping each other in various learning centers throughout the room. The busy hum of activity indicates the children are communicating as they share ideas and interests, work toward solutions to common problems, seek help for individual needs, and, perhaps most important of all, interact socially.

Since the teacher is not to be located in "her station" at the front of the room, the visitor's eye scans the scene to discover her seated with a group of three children who are in the writing center to do their creative writing for the day. They are trying to interpret the springtime color green as creatively as possible. Their inspiration came from a selection the teacher had read earlier in the day and they have asked her to help them now as they try to use descriptive terms to reflect the emotional tones that a color excites. In response to the observer's question, the teacher explains that she had read to the entire group an excerpt from *Hailstones and Halibut Bones.*[2] This beautiful children's book about colors can be used by an innovative teacher to increase perceptual awareness of the environment and to stimulate language development. The teacher had deliberately chosen to use the selection on green as a means of enhancing language expression because it related to the chosen theme for study. It is very apparent that in her own planning and in anticipating directions the study might take, the teacher is providing adult leadership for skill development, aesthetic appreciation, and perceptual awareness as a natural accompaniment to the on-going activities.

In planning the learning environment, the teacher and children have made use of museum and other community resources to create this month's beauty center which they decided to build around the color green and the springtime theme. The beauty center occupies only a very small area of wall space and a table, both of which are covered by a green fabric designed

[2] Mary O'Neill, *Hailstones and Halibut Bones* (New York: Doubleday and Company, 1961).

and woven at the senior citizens' craft center. The fabric provides the background for some pottery, ceramic figurines, and a painting on loan from the museum. A bouquet of forsythia adds contrast.

A display close by has examples of children's interpretations of spring which they have created with their own choice of media to reflect their aesthetic sensitivity to nature as the season changes. The creative writing which is underway will soon be added to this display.

The attention given by the observer to one child's colorful abstract painting brings the young artist to the visitor's side. The child explains that the idea for the picture evolved from an exploratory trip into the community to survey the possibilities for a service project to beautify the neighborhood. After exploring some sites, the children came back into the school filled with ideas about designing flower beds and selecting appropriate plantings for them. This child, after making several geometric designs for a bed, decided instead to paint his impression of the beauty that might come from the completed project.

A math laboratory close at hand reveals that the children's interest in designs for flower beds is only a part of their broader interest in geometric shapes. The scene in the math laboratory located in a corner of the room where shelves, display area, and storage space are available, gives evidence that children are engaged in a variety of math projects. At the present time, two children are experimenting with geoboards and two others are on the floor constructing polyhedrons from simple units. Four other youngsters are around the table creating geometric designs for their flower beds. There is also evidence that some children have been concerned with kite designs and with the mathematical relationships that exist in a baseball diamond.

At this point, any visitor might be slightly bewildered by the many activities underway, some of which seem related only peripherally, or not at all, to the central theme for study. The teacher's leadership in creative writing has been revealed, but one is curious about her involvement in this maze of activity. Furthermore, a quick survey around the room indicates that there are even more interest and work areas yet to be explored, including a science center which serves as a room divider and a carpeted reading corner where some children are talking together quietly. All kinds of questions arise:

Is there an overall plan for this group of youngsters?
Are all of the activities supposed to relate to the theme?

How can one be sure these children are acquiring the necessary skills? Is their balance of content in such a program?

The teacher provides reassurance as she shares some of her experiences in planning with the children for this particular study and talks about her concept of the integrated curriculum. She explains that "What Are the Effects of the Coming of Spring upon Our Community?" serves as the overarching theme and, even though this topic was initiated spontaneously, the instructional program is carefully structured and organized as a result of teacher-pupil planning. The theme offers opportunities for the students to have experiences in many subject areas. The content is used, however, to provide answers to the questions under study and is not taught in the isolated, compartmentalized manner of the traditional school. Individual interests are being met as each child becomes involved in a sub-topic of particular concern to him. The accompanying chart (Figure 1) shows how the study of some of these sub-topics integrates content from many subject areas. An examination of the chart will reveal that balance of content is achieved naturally, just as balance exists in our day to day living experiences.

The children in this classroom know that they are in school to learn and that the questions they pursue serve as the vehicles for their learning. They are aware that skills are to be acquired and areas of knowledge are to be explored. A continuous evaluation is underway as children use check-lists and other self-evaluative devices individually and with their teacher to record their growth. In this classroom each child keeps simple records of his activities. A form such as the one in Figure 2 is an example of individual record keeping. Daily the child makes brief notes about the type of activity he carries out in each area. This is not to say that he must have experiences in all areas every day, but it is expected that a balance among his activities will be apparent at the end of the week.

While most of the activities relate to the chosen theme, children are also engaged in a variety of tasks to improve work and study skills. Some are pursuing special interest areas. A child who is particularly fascinated with photography spends a part of the day discovering how the camera works. Later he may make an added contribution to the study by photographing the designed flower beds or other community projects. A small group of children is studying sentence patterns trying to find a number of ways to express ideas about the feelings they have in spring. The teacher explains that the children recognized a need for this practice when they evaluated some of their writing and discovered that their sentences all started alike. Some other children are reading books and magazines in a quiet corner.

"What Are the Effects of the Coming of Spring Upon Our Community?"

Sub-topic	Social Studies	Science	Math	Language Arts
How are job opportunities changing?	Concepts of seasonal employment and unemployment	Weather changes and prediction	Graphs of employment patterns	Interviewing local employment service agents
How are recreational activities changing?	Space requirements and facilities needed for local recreational needs	Health habits; exercise; need for sunshine	Baseball statistics	Reading about sports events and sports figures in newspapers, magazines, and books
What effects has spring upon transportation?	Use of tax money to maintain roads	Wheels and runners on vehicles; friction	Relative speeds of various forms of transportation	Studying word origins and spellings: automobile, snowmobile, bicycle
How do our foods vary in the spring?	Interdependence of people in various parts of the world; people involved in getting food from source to table	Relation of agriculture to geography and climate	Distances involved from crop source to market	Learning summary and organization skills by making food chart; studying advertising techniques
How is our community changing in appearance?	Moods of people; spring clean-up activities	Changes in nature	Costs of painting; seed costs and amounts needed	Using different vocabulary, sentence patterns, and literary forms to express moods, sights, and sounds of spring

Figure 1.   Integration of Subject Matter

Name _____ Week of _____

Activity	Monday	Tuesday	Wednesday	Thursday	Friday
Arts and Crafts					
Reading					
Writing					
Math					
Theme or Unit Work					
Special Interest					

*The weekly records are kept in a separate folder for each child, along with samples of creative writing, painting, work card activities, and other pupil products. These are used for the purpose of evaluating progress and reporting to parents.

Figure 2.   Weekly Record of Activities

In this classroom, reading skills are developed through reading just as the young photographer is developing research skills as he uses reference books to investigate the principles of the operation of a camera. The visitor becomes aware that skills are being acquired through on-going experiences based upon children's interests as well as through specifically planned lessons that have evolved from diagnosed needs.

This teacher has also developed individually planned lessons in the form of work cards. Each card includes a number of tasks that a child can perform to develop a concept or skill. Children move from simple to complex tasks through the use of a series of cards. Math cards, for example, are organized around the development of skills in linear measurement and exchanging money for goods. An example of a work card used to develop research skills is presented in Figure 3. The child uses the cards on a self-selection basis as a result of his planning with the teacher about his needs. The cards are located in labeled pockets on a bulletin board or in a file box in the related work or interest center.

A student from the nearby university is working with a group of four youngsters at a table out in the corridor where they are developing a food and map chart. Members of this group have carried out research in their homes and in the community as they have discussed with their parents and with local grocers the arrival of new spring foods. From an examination of package labels the children have learned that fresh fruits and vegetables are now arriving from different geographic areas than those from which the foods came during most of the winter months. The community is gradually becoming more self-sufficient as the local farmers begin to supply the metropolitan markets with foods from their hothouses. For example, rhubarb and tomatoes are grown locally while strawberries, pineapples, and dates are shipped in. On their chart, the children are showing the international, national, and local sources of the foods and are gaining an awareness of interrelationships in the expanding community. A child asks whether some of the locally grown foods are now shipped out of their metropolitan area to markets in other states or countries. This question is illustrative of the flow and continuity of learning experiences in an open classroom, for one can see that the question posed could lead to a whole new problem for study.

A committee of three youngsters has been on special assignment in the community and is now returning to the school accompanied by a para-professional who is the mother of one of the children in the room. This committee has had a follow-up meeting with the Director of Parks and

1. Write a question of your own about bicycles or choose one of the following questions that is of interest to you.

   What does the word "bicycle" mean?

   How have bicycles changed in appearance since they were invented?

   What are some of the newest features on bicycles?

   Why are some types of bicycles more expensive than others?

2. Write down two or three sources of information that might be useful in answering the question you have chosen.

   Would any of the following be helpful?

   Dictionary
   Encyclopedia
   Newspaper
   Library book
   Interview
   Others?

3. If you were to use an encyclopedia or dictionary to answer the question, what are some of the topics under which you would look?

4. If you were to use a library book, under what topic headings might you look in the card catalog?

5. Look for the answer to your question in the two or three sources you think would be most useful. Write down the name of each source and write in your own words what you found out in each one.

6. Write a feature article for the newspaper or bulletin board that tells others what you found.

Figure 3.   Work Card to Develop Research Skills

Recreation to discuss the completed plans for the layout of a flower bed in a designated area at the edge of the business district. This activity is a part of the class's project to beautify the community. Another outcome of this effort is that the children are becoming increasingly aware of the role of government in their lives as they have contacts with tax-supported agencies. Concepts about community helpers are expanded through such experiences.

The visitor is invited to the all-purpose room to observe a pre-planned activity that involves the entire class. As the music and physical education teachers arrive, the classroom teacher explains that the three of them have been planning with the children some experiences in movement, rhythm, and song developed around a spring theme. Over a period of time the boys and girls have been interpreting spring through creative dramatics. They have freely interpreted the movements of birds, clouds, kites, and weather. They have chosen songs related to their movements and, in some cases, created their own songs to enhance their interpretations. Today the children are going to portray the rhythm of spring rains and depict in song the moods created. One group of boys has expressed particular interest in illustrating the movements and sounds of a sudden spring storm and is working with a student teacher on this activity.

The principal of the building, who maintains close contact with all phases of the instructional program and who frequently serves as a resource person or teacher's associate, now appears and invites the visitor for coffee. On the way the principal suggests that they stop by the classroom again for a closer look at the science center which the children have developed around their theme. As they enter the room the principal points out that the location of the center as a room divider helps to separate the science laboratory from other work areas.

The science center is attractively arranged with local resources from the community and from the school's instructional materials center. Among the community resources are contributions from the children themselves and from local people who have become interested in the project. A local gardener, who has served as a resource person, has contributed seeds, plants, and instructional material for the planting and cultivation of flowers. A senior high school science teacher has loaned his bird collection to the center. Weather charts have been obtained from the weather bureau; one child has brought some weather instruments from home; and the class has established its own weather service to the school. A previewer on loan from the instructional materials center is used by individuals to gain information from filmstrips on weather and other topics related to the theme.

In the science center, books from many sources are openly and attractively displayed. In addition to science books, there are poetry books to spur children's sensitivity to weather and to help them become aware of the authors' use of language to describe sights and sounds of spring. The colorful verbs and complementary illustrations in *Rain Drop Splash*[3] create a beautiful literary and visual portrayal of the water cycle. Boys in the class can identify with the lad in *Going Barefoot*[4] who envies the rabbits, birds, bees, ants, and frogs while he waits impatiently for June so he too can wear feet bare. Other types of fiction books offer the possibility for children to develop an awareness of how weather affects the lives of people in various parts of the world. The crew of the Kon-Tiki battles severe weather during its voyage in the Pacific;[5] spring festival time in a Swiss village is described in *A Bell for Ursli*;[6] and a migrant family travels from Florida northward as the crops ripen in *Roosevelt Grady*.[7] The teacher obviously is aware that various types of books can add new dimensions to a topic and can also help children become more aware of the world community.

Back in the principal's office as coffee is shared, the visitor tries to summarize his impressions of this program he has observed. Although one day's visit cannot give a total picture, this experience illustrates that a relatively simple and fairly common theme can be developed with sufficient breadth and depth to serve a variety of interests and to develop skills, concepts, generalizations, and attitudes. Even in this brief visit one can see evidences of a great amount of planning and structuring of the learning environment by the teacher and pupils as they work toward commonly defined goals and seek help from others as needs arise. Many inexpensive or readily obtainable resources are utilized as activities are carried out in the classroom,

---

[3] Alvin Tresselt, *Rain Drop Splash* (New York: Lothrop, Lee and Shepard, 1946).

[4] Aileen Fisher, *Going Barefoot* (New York: Thomas Y. Crowell Company, 1960).

[5] Thor Heyerdahl, *Kon-Tiki* (Skokie, Illinois: Rand McNally and Company, 1950).

[6] Selina Chonz, *A Bell for Ursli* (New York: Henry Z. Walck, Inc., 1953).

[7] Louisa R. Shotwell, *Roosevelt Grady* (Cleveland: The World Publishing Company, 1963).

the school, and the community. The visitor notes that an integrated curriculum is achieved as the children use content and skills to answer the questions they have raised. These young citizens are becoming more perceptive about the real world and are making their contribution to the community through their service projects.

THE AREAS OF CONCERN ARE ALLEVIATED

This community-centered curriculum in action gives some evidence that the concerns described in Chapter I are taken into account in an instructional setting built around the needs and interests of children. A cooperatively planned learning laboratory stimulates children to become actively involved in exploring their surroundings. The use of a thematic approach in this setting encourages: individualized instruction, positive self-concepts, creative expression, perceptual awareness, problem-solving, student involvement in planning, language and concept development, and social sensitivity. (See Figure 4.) The following brief discussion presents some of the ways in which the program described in this chapter alleviates these concerns and creates relevancy in the curriculum.

Providing for Individualized Instruction

Many examples of individualized instruction are evident in the scene described. The study, "What Are the Effects of the Coming of Spring upon Our Community?" evolved spontaneously around the interests and experiences of learners. The content was organized around the children's topics and questions, and various sub-topics were identified according to the interests of individuals in the group. The scope of the problem was sufficiently broad to provide for the two boys who had their own special areas of interest and who wanted only to study sports and spring training. Throughout this study each individual interacts with persons and things around him. He takes advantage of the rich learning environment which includes a variety of work and interest centers developed around the theme. The learning laboratory sketched in Figure 5 suggests a way in which the space can be utilized to serve children as they pursue their varied interests.

The process as well as the content of learning is individualized in this classroom. Each child has individualized learning experiences in a variety of work patterns. At times he is working alone in an activity that is of concern only to him, while at other times he is in a tutorial situation in which his teacher or another resource person is providing some help. Sometimes

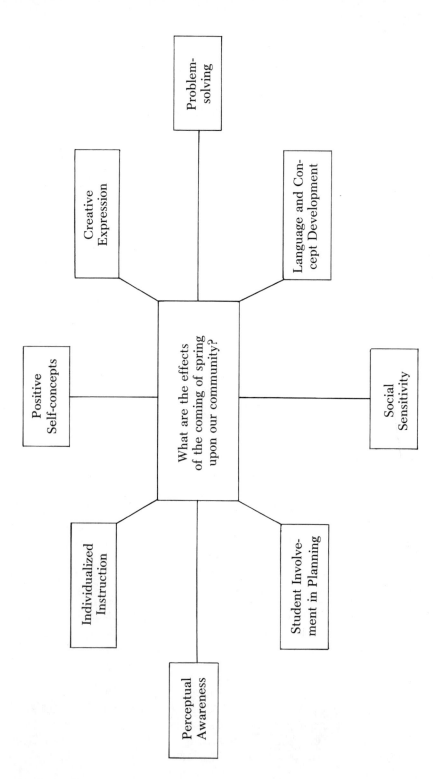

Figure 4.   The Scope of an Integrated Curriculum

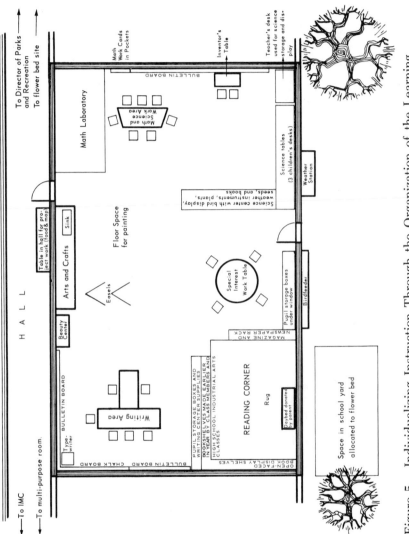

Figure 5. Individualizing Instruction Through the Organization of the Learning Laboratory.

he is with one or more of his peers as they work in teams or in small groups on similar projects in one of the work or interest centers. Sometimes he is functioning as a member of a committee that has been established to carry out a planned activity. And, finally, he contributes and learns as an individual member of a large group when the entire class is pursuing a common goal. Specific examples for each of these work patterns are given in the accompanying chart (Figure 6).

Numerous activities and resources are available to meet individual needs so that each child can learn in many ways. In this setting the teacher works very closely with each pupil in skill development, and evaluation is an on-going process. Because of the wide variety of resources and activities, each child is free to grow at his own rate and is not restricted or frustrated by a single standard of achievement for the class.

Developing a Positive Self-Concept

All of the elements of the instructional program that provide for individualizing learning also enhance the development of a positive self-concept. As the children in the classroom communicate and interact socially and share their home experiences, they develop good feelings about themselves. They do not have some of the fears and anxieties that children often experience in a more closed and teacher-directed environment. They are not afraid to make mistakes and are sufficiently secure to seek help from others as needs arise. The teacher serves as a helper and guide while the children experience the satisfaction that comes from successful progress toward their goals.

Encouraging Creative Expression

Opportunities for creativity abound in an open classroom. Self-expression and divergent thinking are encouraged in this learning laboratory which includes beauty centers, arts and crafts areas, and displays of children's work. The lure to explore uses of equipment in the science center, the challenge to create geometric designs in the math laboratory, and the opportunity to express one's thoughts creatively in the writing area all encourage children to interpret concepts through their own choice of media. As these teachers work cooperatively and integrate content from many specialized areas to enhance the theme for study, the children have more avenues for creative thought than in a subject-centered program. When the physical education and music teachers team with the classroom teacher to

A child needs to have freedom, opportunity, and a place to go to work on his own ideas . . .

. . . or perhaps to sit and think . . .

Work Patterns	Illustrations
Individual effort	Child uses work cards Young photographer studies camera
Teacher-pupil interaction	Child confers with teacher about self-evaluation form Teacher helps child find information on word origins
Team or small group	Children experiment with geoboards Children interpret color in creative writing
Committee	Committee visits Director of Parks and Recreation Committee works in corridor on food and map chart
Large group	Class plans the topic for study Class engages in creative dramatics, rhythms, movement, and songs

Figure 6.   Individualizing Instruction Through the Use of Various Work Patterns

correlate dramatics, movement, rhythms, and songs, these children have a broader range for expression. The music teacher might have limited her contribution to helping children create spring songs. In the team effort, however, she added her insights to those of her colleagues and, through an integrated approach, children were able to create background music to enhance a spontaneous dramatic interpretation. Creativity permeates this curriculum as alert teachers work with children in a flexible and stimulating learning environment.

Increasing Perceptual Awareness

This natural setting for learning which provides a fusion of home and school experiences encourages students to share perceptions about the world around them. When youngsters become more fully involved in the life of the community they develop increased perceptual awareness and become more discriminating in their value judgments as they make decisions. The service project to beautify the community enables youngsters to become more perceptive about the aesthetic elements in their environment, to explore possibilities for the creation of beauty spots, and to visualize designs and colors that would be appropriate. The ability to make such value judgments is based upon a number of perceptual experiences planned by the teacher. In this classroom setting, the reading of the selection from the book *Hailstones and Halibut Bones*[8] encouraged a small group of children to extend their understandings of the color green. Other sensory perceptions such as kinesthetic and auditory were stimulated when the children portrayed the movements of winds and kites and when they responded to the sounds of spring rains. When the development of perceptual awareness is of primary concern, children can interpret the world as they see it and build upon those interpretations as their curiosity is stimulated.

Learning Problem-Solving Skills

Children in the classroom visited are learning problem-solving skills as their study evolves. They are free to raise questions, to plan procedures, to carry out activities, and to make use of a variety of materials in the process. They learn to identify problems and to carry out research as they explore possible solutions. The young photographer was curious about the operation of his camera. He visited a commercial photographer who

[8] Mary O'Neill, *op. cit.*

107

provided him with some information and gave him some printed materials which he took back to the school. He was learning work and study skills in a functional way from on-going experiences built around his interests. To help other children develop problem-solving skills, specifically planned lessons are provided to meet diagnosed needs. In addition, work cards are available to encourage individual students to progress at their own rates. Thus it is evident that the use of a unit approach and some organized steps in planning provide meaningful acquisition of problem-solving skills.

Involving Students in Planning

As youngsters progress through the steps of a unit of work, they become increasingly skilled in cooperative planning. In the beginning pupils assume responsibility for rather simple and clearly defined tasks. The youngsters in the classroom observed have progressed from these early experiences with planning to more advanced stages of self-direction. They have reached the point where an integrated unit has evolved from cooperative planning around a spontaneously developed theme.

Providing for Language and Concept Development

Language develops when communication is permitted and encouraged. Interaction of learners in problem-solving situations is essential to language development. The children who are studying the effects of spring are encouraged to interact with their peers and with the resource people who guide them in their study. For example, these children are developing skills of interviewing by practicing in the classroom and using a tape recorder to evaluate their interviewing techniques. This teacher provides numerous opportunities for children to perfect their communication skills through planned growth activities and through direct contacts.

The learning laboratory with its great variety of materials and activities stimulates concept development. The children who are studying food patterns are developing concepts about movement of goods, supply and demand, and other factors that relate to the costs and distribution of food. Most of the youngsters are developing concepts about weather, growth of plants, and effects of color on the lives of people. In essence, all of the learning activities are leading toward the development of concepts with each learner acquiring ever greater depths of understanding through his own logically organized sequence of experiences.

Developing Social Sensitivity

In the classroom described, children *do* talk in school. Teachers and learners are *not* isolated. The principal is sensitive to his staff and their needs; teachers, in turn, are sensitive to children's perceptions and reactions. An atmosphere of appreciation and concern for others exists and a sense of community evolves. This feeling for others extends beyond the school as youngsters make contacts with senior citizens, city officials, local merchants, and other resource people. A respect for human relationships and interdependencies is learned by the children through such interaction and, furthermore, the people in the community also gain deeper understandings of the school and its instructional program.

A RELEVANT CURRICULUM EMERGES

The cooperative relationships in the open learning environment described in this chapter have developed over an extended period of time. Children are relating home, school, and community experiences and are acquiring attitudes, appreciations, and social learnings. Areas of knowledge are integrated. Children are developing skills in meaningful contexts. The topics for study have originated from the firsthand experiences of the boys and girls, and many activities are carried out as a multi-media approach is used. Responsible behavior is gradually being learned through a series of carefully planned experiences. As these children study the world that is known to them, they become increasingly aware of their roles in an expanding community and a relevant curriculum emerges.

CHAPTER VII

**TEACHER EDUCATION FOR A
COMMUNITY-CENTERED CURRICULUM**

Teacher Education For A Community-Centered Curriculum

Curriculum revision which results in integrated studies carried out in a community-school setting depends upon knowledgeable and skilled teachers. However, teachers teach as they were taught — and they were not taught in community-centered schools; therefore, major revisions are necessary in both pre-service and in-service teacher education programs. It is imperative that the university faculty cooperate with the local school systems to provide an experience curriculum for teachers in which the community is used as a learning laboratory.

AN EXPERIENCE PROGRAM FOR TEACHERS

If teachers are to function effectively in an integrated curriculum, they must experience the approaches to learning that they will be using with children. A teacher who has never experienced individualized instruction cannot be expected to provide an individualized program for youngsters. Merely discussing these procedures in methods classes is not sufficient.

A teacher needs to feel that her total educational program has been planned specifically for her and that her professional experiences within the curriculum are also individualized. Thus, for each participant the teacher education program must provide:

1. firsthand experiences with children.

2. firsthand experiences in the community.

3. experiences that will enhance the teacher's self-concept.

4. early experiences that will orient prospective teachers to the profession and help them to make a decision about teaching as a career.

5. experiences that will help teachers increase their perceptual awareness of environmental problems in the community setting.

6. a multi-media approach.

7. a wide variety of learning activities and methods.

8. experiences that will help teachers to see relationships among the subject fields and enable them to integrate content areas.

9. experiences that will help teachers to develop work and study skills, arouse curiosity, see a need to ask questions, seek answers, and evaluate and apply findings.

10. opportunities to develop social sensitivity in relationships with fellow students, faculty, pupils in the schools, and community resource people.

A teacher education program which includes these components can be designed to individualize learning, to develop problem-solving skills, and to orient teachers to a community-centered curriculum.

PROBLEM-SOLVING AT THE COLLEGE LEVEL

Prospective teachers who help to plan their professional programs in a redesigned teacher education curriculum will become skilled in using problem-solving approaches. The experiences they have will promote an awareness of the realities of teaching and will encourage them to solve problems they have identified.

But teachers must be guided to develop problem-solving skills. A gradual approach to problem-solving is as necessary at the college level as it is in working with younger students. As a matter of fact, more patience and skill are required to help college students develop problem-solving abilities because these older students have had many school experiences which have conditioned them to the traditional methods of education. Even with today's clamor for involvement, students who are urged by their instructors to share in decision-making in the college classroom are often openly embarrassed about their inabilities to plan and organize cooperatively. They *expect* to listen to lectures; they want their instructors to assume the initiative for planning and organizing course content and method. It is only after they have gained a feeling of security and confidence that they assume any major responsibility for their learning.

To bring about some change in attitude and to develop skills in problem-solving, prospective teachers should have the opportunity to know well and to work closely with at least one faculty member for an extended time. Over a period of years, large blocks of time should be allocated for this purpose. Furthermore, college students should have the experience of working on a continuing basis with a faculty team.

The planning principles that apply in the community-centered classroom should also apply in the teacher education setting. For example, the development of rapport between students and faculty is as important at the higher education level as in the elementary and secondary settings. College students, too, need opportunities to view others as real persons who are acceptant and who have empathic understanding.[1]

Early in the college program when the student has tentatively identified with teacher education, exploratory opportunities should be provided. Just as an orientation unit can be used early in the elementary or secondary community-school classroom, a similar unit can also be used to initiate college students into their programs. The orientation should introduce the prospective teacher to the current educational scene—to learners, to the organization of educational programs, to the role of the teacher and other school personnel, to classroom and community settings, and to problems and issues with which education is concerned. Through such experiences students will identify special areas of interest and become acquainted with the teaching profession. They can pursue further study as they investigate individual and group problems.

---

[1] Carl R. Rogers, "The Interpersonal Relationship in the Facilitation of Learning," in *Humanizing Education: The Person in the Process* (Washington, D.C.: Association for Supervision and Curriculum Development, 1967), pp. 1-18.

As areas for study are identified, college students will be working with faculty members to develop cooperative planning skills. They will need to develop objectives, define scope, make use of a multi-media approach, carry out a variety of activities, and evaluate in terms of the objectives established. Careful attention must be given to each of these steps in problem-solving. Individualized programs are not haphazard and they require much more effort than group instruction. To cite an example, an individual or group of college students might become concerned about the inappropriate curriculum for inner-city children. The prospective teachers could work cooperatively with local teachers and university faculty members to define the problem, develop hypotheses, plan to find evidence from a variety of sources, and finally apply their findings with some inner-city children.

In a flexibly organized teacher education program which provides individualized instruction, course sequences and course descriptions cannot be prescribed. If prospective teachers are to become skilled in cooperative planning and in problem-solving, they must have many types of experiences in which they help to determine the course content and select activities appropriate to their needs. It is essential that faculty teams plan cooperatively with students to develop meaningful, individualized programs.

Most teacher education programs do not yet provide the flexible structure suggested here. In the process of moving toward a more individualized approach, cooperative planning can be introduced in traditional courses. However certain limitations must be anticipated. Students in college classes which meet once or twice a week for a semester have difficulty developing rapport and using teacher-pupil planning techniques because of the short class periods and the time that elapses between meetings. Under such circumstances, a period for orientation and the development of good working relationships may extend for almost three-fourths of the semester. Often it is only toward the end of the course that students indicate their willingness to explore cooperative planning approaches. On the other hand, students in classes meeting on a daily basis express a desire to advance with cooperative planning much earlier in the term. Because of these problems a college faculty might want to study methods of scheduling classes for more frequent contacts. Another possible arrangement might allow a faculty member or team to have continuing contact with a particular group of college students for a period extending beyond the usual term or semester. Greater flexibility in the schedule permits time to plan and use community resources more extensively.

116

In graduate classes and in-service educational programs, experienced teachers, too, can develop problem-solving skills and engage in cooperative planning. The pattern of the typical graduate class meeting one evening a week for a lecture or discussion in a barren college classroom is not conducive to helping teachers become skilled in implementing a community-centered curriculum. College faculty and public school educators must cooperate in planning learning experiences for prospective and experienced teachers in community-school settings.

In-service programs for teachers may be planned around the problem: How Can Our Community Be Used as a Learning Laboratory? A Community-Classroom Workshop can be developed around this theme and can be carried out in *any* community — rural, inner-city, or suburban. College consultants can serve with teachers on a planning committee and then, as the workshop is in progress, they can help teachers develop resource units and make use of a multi-media approach. Such programs take the university professor away from the college campus and bring him into a closer working relationship with classroom teachers and the community. As a result, all participants are helped to see the relationships between theory and practice.

The Community-Classroom Workshop should utilize all kinds of resources within the community, not just those associated with business and industry. Teachers should have firsthand experiences to improve their perceptual awareness of the local surroundings. If they are to encourage pupils to look at the familiar for new insights, they should engage in many of the same types of activities they might later expect to carry out with their students. Teachers should go out to explore the community, talk with resource people, visit historical sites, and take pictures to share with other workshop participants. Later the pupils in their classrooms should be given the same privileges of exploring and recording events of interest and significance to them. Teachers should not impose their perceptions of the community and the photographs they took earlier. Even though workshop activities enable the teacher to have the same kinds of learning experiences that children will have, these experiences must not substitute for the first-hand involvement of the students. The teachers must realize that the skills they are learning in the workshop are just as important as the understandings they are gaining about the community. Having experienced problem-solving approaches themselves, they will be more capable of helping their pupils acquire similar skills.

A LEARNING LABORATORY FOR TEACHERS

In most teacher education programs prospective teachers have been boxed into dull, uninspiring classrooms and have been isolated from the outside world for which their education is supposedly preparing them.

In order to prepare teachers for a community-centered curriculum, a learning laboratory that integrates theory and practice is essential. Direct experiences with children should occur in the community setting. As an example, a university faculty team and a group of prospective teachers may use a section of the inner-city as a learning laboratory. Through cooperation between the university and the local school system a space in one of the schools serves as the center for learning. Firsthand experiences with youngsters in the community and in community schools provide the problems for study. Thus a community-centered learning laboratory is established. Another type of learning laboratory can be provided to take advantage of the community which is located in a special setting.

The Community in a Special Setting: Colonial Williamsburg

One example of a learning laboratory in a special setting is the Workshop in Early American Life which is held in Colonial Williamsburg each August. For several years Eastern Michigan University in close cooperation with Colonial Williamsburg and the College of William and Mary has conducted a two-week program to provide teachers with firsthand learning experiences in a historical setting.

The Williamsburg Workshop is designed to help teachers become familiar with community resources and to consider ways in which they can use similar resources in their own classrooms. Teachers become aware of the interrelationships among subject disciplines in the community setting. The workshop at first appears to be a historical study; however, as insights are gained, participants recognize that art, music, home economics, industrial arts, geography, archeology, and many other content areas are represented. Teachers consider the many different ways in which historical sites can be used as learning centers, and they develop skills in preparing and using resource units through a multi-media approach. [2]

---

[2] For a description of this workshop, see Wilma Russell, "Journey to Williamsburg," *The Elementary School Journal* 69 (January, 1969), pp. 186-191.

Teacher Education for a Community-Centered Curriculum

A Multi-Media Approach in a Special Setting

Resource people from many specialized areas are available to talk with the participants in the Williamsburg Workshop. As these individuals discuss and demonstrate their interest areas, a close working relationship among the resource people and an interdependence in special areas is readily apparent to the learners. These interrelationships are reinforced as the workshop participants experience many different types of activities. They hear lectures, participate in discussions, view demonstrations, see slides and films, take field trips, interview resource people, and view special collections and historical buildings. Teachers explore the possibilities for using their own communities as learning laboratories. Divergent thinking and inquiry techniques are emphasized.

As a result of these experiences, the teachers develop resource materials and resource units. They become familiar with a variety of materials and activities which enable them to make use of a multi-media approach to learning in their own home communities and classrooms. In reality, every community is a historical site that can serve as a laboratory for an integrated curriculum.

Perhaps an illustration can serve to suggest some ways in which resources in the community can stimulate a variety of learnings. Workshop members become increasingly aware of the fences in Williamsburg. They are stimulated to look at the variations of fence designs, materials, locations, and to account for the differences that are noted. This learning experience also utilizes an inquiry approach which extends beyond the mere study of fences to involve the observers in raising questions about the lives of the people who made use of the fences. The interdisciplinary relationships become apparent as this study draws upon such subjects as history, fine arts, geography, and sociology. The insights gained from the attention to fences result from guided tours, individual walks, viewing slides, and interacting with resource people. A textbook approach cannot begin to sharpen the observation skills and stimulate the thinking powers as can these multi-media activities.

A walk or field trip which provides a learning experience for teachers in a special setting has carry-over into the classroom and suggests ideas for introducing some multi-media approaches. For example, a similar walk for children is possible in the home community. A walk in which attention is centered on fences, shapes, colors, movements, or sounds can increase awareness and encourage divergent thinking. Direct experience can be supplemented with the use of other media. For example, films, slides,

As learners become aware of the fences in Williamsburg, they may also be stimulated to look at architectural features and at garden designs and plantings. Relationships between the man-made and the natural environment can be identified. Scenes will be different, but similar opportunities for learning exist in a local community.

and tape recordings made during the walk can be taken back into the classroom and used as the basis for many language activities. The use of multi-media has become an integral part of the experience, and the activity that began as a walk to look at fences in Williamsburg has now developed into an enriched program for boys and girls.

AN INTEGRATED CURRICULUM FOR TEACHERS

Teachers who are expected to implement an integrated curriculum with their pupils must have some experience with this approach in their preparation or in-service programs. How is an integrated curriculum provided in the community-centered approach to teacher education? In the first place, the teachers are in a learning laboratory in which materials, content, and activities are integrated in a problem-solving situation. Prospective teachers who are studying and working in a community setting such as the inner-city will experience an integration of theory and practice as they see principles of learning reflected in the observed behaviors of children. Further, the various content areas are integrated around a common theme or problem. An integration of individual and group activities results when the total program is planned and developed through cooperative team work.

The opportunity to interact with people having a wide range of back-grounds and interests is deemed to be a strength—indeed an essential component—of a teacher education program. When prospective and in-service teachers are exposed only to courses in their own specialized areas such as reading, music, or science, they lack a broad perspective. Thus it is advisable that college students and faculty members comprise hetero-geneous groups so there will be interaction among members who have special areas of interest and are concerned with children of different age groups. In addition, their experiences and activities should include contacts with children from many different backgrounds and socio-economic levels. The teacher education curriculum suggested in this chapter does permit individuals and small groups to develop in-depth projects along special lines of interest but these must be viewed as they relate to the total program. The planning team has the responsibility for balancing general education and special interest activities into an integrated curriculum for teachers.

A TEAM APPROACH TO LEARNING

A team approach is essential to undergraduate programs and to in-service programs such as the Community-Classroom Workshop and the Williamsburg Workshop. These programs involve faculty members, resource people, and learners in continuous and cooperative planning which is more than team teaching—it is a team approach to *learning* and the focus is on the *learner*.

At the undergraduate level, the team approach can be used in working with a group of prospective teachers in a block-of-time. A faculty team can plan a series of activities with the students that will provide experiences in the schools, in the community, and in the university setting. A flexible schedule is essential. Some grouping of prospective teachers for discussions and other activities is necessary, and some time is reserved for independent study.

Because of the need for individualizing instruction and the differences in learning styles, a variety of activities is important at both graduate and undergraduate levels. The focus must be on the learner and on his learning experiences instead of on the teacher and the teaching methods. The teacher must be concerned with creating a stimulating environment. When the lecture and other traditionally teacher dominated activities are used, the community-centered curriculum cannot be achieved in teacher education or in the elementary and secondary schools. This does not imply that the classroom teacher or the university professor abdicates his responsibility, but it does mean that he assumes a different kind of responsibility. His role is to provide leadership, act as a facilitator of learning, and serve as a resource person. University faculty members engaged in team work with prospective teachers must develop skills in:

1. initiating discussions.
2. asking questions that lead to divergent thinking.
3. planning with students and resource people.
4. arranging and carrying out a variety of activities.
5. stimulating creativity.
6. recognizing and solving problems.

INDIVIDUALIZING INSTRUCTION

Prospective and experienced teachers come to their professional preparation with varied educational backgrounds and many different contacts with children and schools. Teacher education programs must be individualized so that they build upon the past experiences of each learner and provide new experiences in unexplored areas. Students must pursue selected courses and independent studies according to their needs and interests.

In an integrated curriculum prospective teachers can become acquainted with community life, work with small groups of children, and assist teachers in the classroom and community settings. These experiences require pre-planning, organization, and guidance so that learners achieve their purposes and maximal benefits are obtained. Unless these participation and pre-student teaching experiences are planned and carried out as integral parts of an individual's program, they are of limited value.

Individual in-depth studies are an essential part of all teacher education programs. In the undergraduate curriculum or in workshops and other types of in-service activities, special projects and in-depth studies will be planned and carried out. A primary teacher, for example, might be interested in the development of visual and motor coordination of young children. A compilation of suggestions about the use of natural activities in the classroom and community to develop coordination skills might result from an in-depth investigation. If such studies are to have relevance they, too, must evolve as a result of planning which has occurred in the team approach to learning. Prospective teachers must engage in long-range planning in their own programs and in their teaching contacts with pupils. In both situations attention must be given to establishing objectives, carrying out activities, and evaluating results.

EVALUATING THE TEACHER EDUCATION PROGRAM

Individualizing instruction in a learning laboratory for teachers requires participants to assume some responsibility. Having set the directions for their programs and having participated in organizational planning, these teachers then must assess and evaluate the outcomes. Self-evaluation is essential. In order for them to help their pupils assume the responsibility that must accompany freedom, teachers must experience self-evaluative activities in their own preparation.

With the team approach to learning, ample opportunity is provided for teams of resource people to work with individual students as well as with groups of learners in evaluative sessions. College staff members, prospective teachers, and public school faculties will all share in evaluation of the programs, the groups, and the individuals involved.

Continuous evaluation is needed as prospective teachers engage in a sequence of problem-solving activities. Evaluation of the projects, independent studies, and resource units is carried out until the objectives have been achieved, thus obviating the assignment of grades. Grades are unnecessary at all levels when attention is centered on a consideration of whether the activities are leading to the desired objectives.

University programs, too, must be evaluated in terms of objectives. Such evaluation includes both the undergraduate and graduate programs designed to help teachers implement a community-centered curriculum.

Evaluation extends beyond the campus programs to the in-service workshops. Ultimately, the evaluation will rest upon the extent to which the integrated curriculum of the community-centered school becomes an integral part of the educational system of the United States.

NEW DIRECTIONS IN TEACHER EDUCATION

The teacher education program described in this chapter is not a prescriptive model. If teacher education is to provide a community-centered learning experience for teachers, no model is adequate. Each program must be unique. The community must serve as a learning laboratory in which teachers develop problem-solving skills and make use of multi-media approaches. In this laboratory teachers experience individualized instruction in an integrated curriculum which prepares them to use their communities as classrooms.

BIBLIOGRAPHY

CHILDREN'S BOOKS CITED

Chonz, Selina. *A Bell for Ursli*. New York: Henry Z. Walck, Inc., 1953.

Fisher, Aileen. *Going Barefoot*. New York: Thomas Y. Crowell Company, 1960.

Heyerdahl, Thor. *Kon-Tiki*. Skokie, Illinois: Rand McNally and Company, 1950.

O'Neill, Mary. *Hailstones and Halibut Bones*. New York: Doubleday and Company, 1961.

Shotwell, Louisa R. *Roosevelt Grady*. Cleveland: The World Publishing Company, 1963.

Tresselt, Alvin. *Rain Drop Splash*. New York: Lothrop, Lee and Shepard, 1946.

WORKS CITED

Association for Childhood Education International. *Toward Effective Grouping*. Washington, D. C.: Association for Childhood Education International, 1962.

Association for Supervision and Curriculum Development. *Humanizing Education: The Person in the Process*. Washington, D. C.: National Education Association, 1967.

LaBenne, Wallace D., and Bert I. Greene. *Educational Implications of Self-Concept Theory*. Pacific Palisades, California: Goodyear Publishing Co., Inc., 1969.

Lee, Dorris M., and R. V. Allen. *Learning to Read Through Experience*. Second edition. New York: Appleton-Century-Crofts, 1963.

Martin, Bill, Jr. *The Human Connection*. Washington, D. C.: Department of Elementary-Kindergarten—Nursery Education of the National Education Association, 1967.

Miel, Alice, with Edwin Kiester, Jr. *The Shortchanged Children of Suburbia*. New York: Institute of Human Relations Press, The American Jewish Committee, 1967.

Report of the National Advisory Commission on Civil Disorders. New York: New York Times Co., 1968.

Rosenthal, Robert, and Lenore Jacobson. *Pygmalion in the Classroom*. New York: Holt, Rinehart and Winston, Inc., 1968.

Rukare, Enoka H. "Aspirations for Education in the 'New' and Free Nations of Africa," *Educational Leadership* 27 (November, 1969), pp. 124-128.

Russell, Wilma. "Journey to Williamsburg," *The Elementary School Journal* 69 (January, 1969), pp. 186-191.

Taylor, Harold. *The World as Teacher*. Garden City, New York: Doubleday and Company, Inc., 1969.

U. S. Department of Health, Education, and Welfare. Office of Education. *Equality of Educational Opportunity*. Washington, D. C.: Government Printing Office, 1966.

SUGGESTIONS FOR ADDITIONAL REFERENCES

Learners, teachers, and local environments are unique and are ever-changing, thus no packaged curriculum guides or materials can be provided for the development of integrated educational experiences suited to each situation. If a program is prescribed, the curriculum is no longer community-centered nor is it open education. Nonetheless, the teacher who is committed to the use of the community as a classroom can find inspiration, guidelines, and helpful suggestions in a variety of professional references. This bibliography is by no means complete, but is provided as a small sample of the topics that might be investigated and of the types of reference materials that might prove useful in the evolution of a community-centered classroom.

GENERAL PROFESSIONAL REFERENCES AND RESOURCE BOOKS

Ashton-Warner, Sylvia. *Teacher.* New York: Simon and Schuster, 1963.

> A creative, sensitive teacher describes her experiences with Maori children in an infant school in New Zealand. The "organic" reading and writing of these youngsters is based upon their own language and their daily life experiences.

Allen, Roach Van, and Claryce Allen. *Teacher's Resource Book for Language Experiences in Early Childhood.* Chicago: Encyclopedia Britannica Educational Corporation, 1969.

> A source of creative ideas to develop communication skills of young children by using their interests and experiences. Many suggestions are made for organizing the classroom and for providing a variety of activities to stimulate sensory awareness of the local environments.

Allen, Roach Van, and Claryce Allen. *Teacher's Resource Book for Language Experiences in Reading.* Volumes I, II, and III. Chicago: Encyclopedia Britannica Educational Corporation, 1966-1970.

> A series of carefully planned learning activities to stimulate functional development of language arts skills through firsthand experiences. Local resources, audio-visual materials, books, and poems are suggested for a variety of topics ranging from "Plastics" to "Exploring Wildlife Around Us" to "Work-Yesterday, Today and Tomorrow." Excellent, readily usable ideas to help the teacher move into an integrated curriculum.

Blackie, John. *Inside the Primary School.* London: Her Majesty's Stationery Office, 1967.

> An easy-to-read presentation of the principles underlying changes in the British primary schools and of some practical applications of those principles. After explaining how children learn, the role of teachers and the organization of the school, Blackie describes each of the subject areas as part of the integrated curriculum and offers many examples that could be adapted to schools in the United States.

Brogan, Peggy, and Lorene K. Fox. *Helping Children Read.* New York: Holt, Rinehart and Winston, 1961.

> An introduction to individualized reading written by teachers who were seeking creative, interesting approaches to help children become readers. The authors discuss ways to bring about change in the school, ideas for setting up the classroom, and ways to stimulate children to become authors.

Brown, Mary E., and Norman Precious. *The Integrated Day in the Primary School.* New York: Agathon Press, Inc., 1969.

The headmistress and headmaster of an infant and a junior school in Leicestershire explain the meaning and the development of the integrated day, stressing pupil involvement, discovery, and learning through the natural flow of activity. Excellent, practical ideas for providing a stimulating environment and for relating traditional curriculum areas within the ongoing flow of school life. Includes an appendix of suggested equipment and materials.

Buckeye, Donald A., William A. Ewbank, and John L. Ginther. *Cloudburst of Math Lab Experiments.* Birmingham, Michigan: Midwest Publications Company, Inc., 1971. A resource library of experiments covering both "modern" and "traditional" math. The suggestions in these materials are similar to the work card activities developed by some of the teachers in the British schools.

Darrow, Helen Fisher, and R. Van Allen. *Independent Activities for Creative Learning.* New York: Bureau of Publications, Teachers College, Columbia University, 1961.

A source book of ideas for independent activities that will foster self-expression and divergent thinking. A teacher will find many inexpensive, easily arranged activities that will stimulate the creative responses of children.

Lee, Dorris, and R. V. Allen. *Learning to Read through Experience.* Second edition. New York: Appleton-Century-Crofts, 1963.

An introduction to the language-experience approach showing how children learn listening, speaking, reading, and writing skills as they communicate about their own experiences. Describes an open learning environment and includes a chapter on group and individual activities.

Nesbitt, Marion. *A Public School for Tomorrow.* New York: Dell Publishing Co., Inc., 1967.

A description of a humanized elementary school in Richmond, Virginia, in which the emphasis is upon children and personal interaction. The book includes discussions of the physical adjustments made in an old building, the planning activities of all of the people involved, the opportunities for meaningful learning experiences within the traditional subject areas, and means of improving home-school relationships.

Noar, Gertrude. *Teaching and Learning the Democratic Way.* Englewood Cliffs, New Jersey: Prentice-Hall, 1963.

An extensive discussion of the steps in teacher-pupil planning. The second part of the book contains short resource units on such social concerns as intergroup relations.

Plowden, Lady Bridget, *et al. Children and Their Primary Schools: A Report of the Central Advisory Council for Education England.* Volume I. London: Her Majesty's Stationery Office, 1967.

The detailed report of the status of education in England and the recommendations for further development.

Rogers, Vincent R., editor. *Teaching in the British Primary School.* London: The Macmillan Company, Collier-Macmillan Limited, 1970.

A collection of papers written for Americans by classroom teachers and headmasters in England. The authors speak clearly and with conviction from backgrounds reflecting on-the-spot experiences. One chapter is entitled "Social and Environmental Studies," but the community-classroom concept is reflected in all of the other chapters as well. An excellent comprehensive reference.

Silberman, Charles E. *Crisis in the Classroom.* New York: Random House, 1970.

A detailed, critical examination and analysis of the problems in American education, followed by an extensive discussion of how school programs from preschool years through teacher education levels might be improved. Includes a chapter on the English schools and another chapter describing changes underway in various U.S. schools. A thought provoking report touching upon a wide range of matters pertinent to "the remaking of American education."

Veatch, Jeannette. *Reading in the Elementary School.* New York: The Ronald Press Company, 1966.

A complete professional text by one of the leading proponents of individualized reading. Suggests gradual steps for teachers wishing to move into new patterns of teaching reading. Has lengthy chapter on establishing interest centers for the independent work period. Other features include guidelines for conducting conferences and for keeping records, suggestions for skill development, and a description of the integration of reading with the traditional content areas.

Waskin, Yvonne, and Louise Parrish, *Teacher-Pupil Planning.* New York: Pitman Publishing Corporation, 1967.

Emphasizes a variety of approaches to teacher-pupil planning. Geared toward junior high, but can be adapted to all levels. Many helpful guidelines for such areas as getting acquainted, beginning in planning, techniques of cooperative evaluation, human relations, the teacher's role, and teacher-pupil planning in the world scene.

Wright, Betty Atwell, *et al. Elementary School Curriculum: Better Teaching Now.* New York: The Macmillan Company, 1971.

A basic textbook on building a dynamic curriculum for today's children. The authors present implications of psychology, sociology, and philosophy for developing a life management and social action curriculum. Illustrations of actual learning situations as well as suggestions for further applications are found throughout the book.

PAMPHLETS AND BROCHURES

Association for Childhood Education International. *Involvement Bulletin Boards.* Washington, D. C.: Association for Childhood Education International, 1970.

One way for a teacher to begin to move toward teacher-pupil planning is to devise bulletin boards to which children can relate and respond. The ideas in this pamphlet could serve as starters, after which the teacher and pupils could plan some open-ended bulletin boards of their own.

The British Infant School. I/D/E/A/'s Early Childhood Series, Volume One. Melbourne, Florida: Institute for Development of Educational Activities, Inc., 1969.

A colorful occasional paper by I/D/E/A/ which is a summary of an international seminar of educators who observed and discussed innovations in British primary schools. The booklet has brief descriptions of family grouping, the integrated day, materials, play yards, and record keeping, and includes diagrams of two simple classroom arrangements.

Featherstone, Joseph. *The Primary School Revolution in Britain.* Reprints of three articles from *The New Republic* of August 10, September 2, and September 9, 1967. New York: Pitman Publishing Corporation.

An excellent and often cited summary of developments in primary schools in England. Featherstone describes his impressions and observations clearly and vividly in the three articles: "Schools for Children: What's Happening in British Classrooms;" "How Children Learn;" "Teaching Children to Think." Many practical helps.

Kenworthy, Leonard S. *The International Dimension of Education.* Washington, D. C.: Association for Supervision and Curriculum Development, NEA, 1970.

In this background paper prepared for the 1970 ASCD World Conference on Education, Kenworthy describes the world of the foreseeable future and tells why internationally-minded individuals are needed. He proposes a curriculum with international dimensions and makes suggestions for themes and activities at elementary, secondary, and college levels. Includes a short chapter on methods and resources for learning to live internationally.

Moyer, Joan E., *Bases for World Understanding and Cooperation: Suggestions for Teaching the Young Child.* Washington, D. C.: Association for Supervision and Curriculum Development, NEA, 1970.

Prepared for the 1970 ASCD World Conference on Education, this pamphlet includes suggestions for helping children under six become world-minded. The emphasis is upon the process of developing human relations through interactions with many people as an integral part of the school curriculum. The generalizations to be developed and the action proposals are appropriate for older children as well. Suggestions are given for promoting growth in perceiving, communicating, loving, knowing, decision making, organizing, creating, and valuing.

Open Education: The Legacy of the Progressive Movement. Washington, D. C.: National Association for the Education of Young Children, 1970.

Analyses of the early American progressive movement and current English open education experiences. Authorities discuss the concept of open education from psychological, sociological, historical, and philosophical perspectives and offer suggestions and challenges regarding the implementation of the concept in today's schools.

Yeoman, Edward. *Education for Initiative and Responsibility.* Boston: National Association of Independent Schools, 1968.

The author's observations and reflections on a visit to some primary schools in Leicestershire in 1967. Appendix V contains a list of recommended equipment for a room of eight to eleven year olds.

JOURNAL ARTICLES

Barth, Roland S. "When Children Enjoy School: Some Lessons from Britain," *Childhood Education* 46 (January, 1970), pp. 195-200.

The Community is the Classroom

An elementary principal from Connecticut analyzes seven reasons underlying a child's enjoyment of school and gives examples of the types of educational experiences that bring about positive attitudes toward learning.

Brown, Julie L. "Our Eighth Graders Tackled Air Pollution," *Today's Education* 59 (February, 1970), pp. 60-61.

The students in a junior-high school English-history class undertake a study of pollution in their community. This article tells of the local resources that were utilized, the types of skills and knowledge acquired by the students, and the effect of the study upon pollution control in the community.

Clegg, Sir Alec. "The Revolution in the English Elementary Schools," 49 *The National Elementary Principal* (September, 1969), pp. 23-32.

The author vividly describes scenes in traditional and new primary schools in England and maintains that the latter are "a joy to visit." He explains how the improvements in schools are of value to children and why the changes are essential to healthy social development.

Clegg, Sir Alec. "What Is a Humanizing Curriculum?" *The National Elementary Principal* 49 (February, 1970), pp. 8-12.

The chief education officer of West Riding, Yorkshire, discusses the features of a humane curriculum that lead youngsters to develop feelings of self-worth and social sensitivity.

Clinchy, Evans. "Good School in a Ghetto," *Saturday Review* 51 (November 16, 1968), pp. 106-107, 118-119.

A condemned building in the middle of Roxbury urban renewal area is the site of a demonstation school in Boston where classrooms have been transformed into learning laboratories and where children are being helped to learn by means of experiences and topics of interest to them. Paraprofessionals from the community serve as teacher assistants. Field trips into the surrounding neighborhood provide inspiration for stories and pictures.

Dixon, Nathaniel R. "Wider Windows for Elementary Schools," *Childhood Education* 47 (February, 1971), pp. 250-253.

A short, idea-packed article telling of the extension of the learning environment of an inner-city school in Washington, D. C. into the community. In the words of Mr. Dixon, ". . . the community became the school . . ."

Grissett, Helen T. "Touch-Feel Learning at Tallahassee Junior Museum," *Childhood Education* 47 (February, 1971), pp. 261-264.

The Tallahassee Junior Museum is a community resource planned specifically for children to have firsthand sensory experiences in social and natural life activities. The Museum functions year-round ". . . . as an extension of the classroom."

Purvis, Susan. "Museums and the Schools," *Today's Education* 57 (December, 1968), pp. 14-17.

Examples of varied uses of museum services in selected parts of the United States. Although most of the programs have not reached the stages of the school museum services in England, there are many ideas for teachers and museum personnel who wish to develop a closer working relationship.

BIBLIOGRAPHIES OF MATERIALS FOR CHILDREN

Association for Childhood Education International. *The World in Children's Picture Books.* Washington, D. C.: Association for Childhood Education International, 1968.

A short bibliography of "some of the most distinguished and appealing picture books" about people and life in many areas of the world, arranged by countries.

Crosby, Muriel, editor. *Reading Ladders for Human Relations.* Fourth Edition. Washington, D. C.: American Council on Education, 1963.

An annotated list of books designed to help readers acquire greater sensitivity to human relations. Each ladder of books includes a range of reading levels and interests from preschool to adult. The books are organized around the following themes: How It Feels to Grow Up; The Individual and the Group; The Search for Values; Feeling at Home in our Country; Feeling at Home in Other Lands; Living with Change; and Living as a Free People.

Huus, Helen, *Children's Books to Enrich the Social Studies.* Washington, D. C.: National Council for Social Studies, 1966.

An annotated bibliography of children's books organized around the main topics of Our World, Times Past, People Today, The World's Work, and Living Together. Children and teachers would find this a helpful resource for locating fiction and non-fiction books about the expanding community in which we live.

Marantz, Kenneth. *A Bibliography of Children's Art Literature.* Washington, D. C.: National Art Education Association, NEA, 1965.

The subtitle is "An Annotated Bibliography of Children's Literature Designed to Stimulate and Enrich the Visual Imagination of the Child." Children and teachers could use this reference to locate books about art and paintings, artists, museums, techniques for various art media, folk art, anthropology, archeology, poetry, alphabet and counting books, and picture books. Teachers will find excellent suggestions for books that will contribute to the development of perceptual awareness and aesthetic sensitivity.

Professional Rights and Responsibilities Committee on Civil and Human Rights of Educators. *An Index to Multi-Ethnic Teaching Materials and Teacher Resources.* Washington, D.C.: PR&R Committee on Civil and Human Rights of Educators, NEA, 1967.

This guide would be useful for teachers planning resource units and desiring to include materials that will promote multi-cultural understandings.